FACES
ON MY
JOURNEY

THE AID FOR FRIENDS STORY

FACES
ON MY
JOURNEY

THE AID FOR FRIENDS STORY

Rita Ungaro-Schiavone

Printed in the United States of America.

Library of Congress Catalog Card Number 93-72893
ISBN 0-9628363-5-4

Dedication

This book is dedicated to Michael Angelo Schiavone, the most perfect husband God has ever blessed a woman with. He is my rock, my friend, my advisor. Mike has always encouraged me and supported my work in the community these past 25 years. He has always been by my side patiently helping me. When I was sick and felt I could no longer continue, he was there to tell me otherwise. Without my husband's encouragement, I would have given up long ago. I thank God for that special blessing.

This book is also dedicated to Dorothy, Freddy, Mary, Catherine, Marian, Cathy, and all of the others I have had the privilege of knowing these past 18 years since I founded Aid For Friends.

CONTENTS

Prologue

Permit me to introduce myself, because who I am is totally relevant to what I am about to write. I am Mike, Rita's husband, and I have been privileged to take many steps on Rita's journey by her side.

As you meet the people in this book and discover their faces, look also for the divine, for it is surely there, shining through all the love, faith, hope, and courage exhibited by all those friends, volunteers, and client-friends alike, who are recorded in the following stories.

I have come to think of Aid For Friends as one of the many modern-day repetitions of the miracle of the loaves and the fishes. To me the parable is not just about the multiplication of the loaves and the fishes; it is about faith. It is about all the wondrous things that can happen when one has deep faith and courage.

I can remember as though it were yesterday that night when Rita and I and our four sons—Mike, Vince, Joe, and Steve—were eating dinner and Rita told us about visiting Minnie. Minnie was blind, bedridden, sweet, and lovely. There was absolutely no food in her house. Rita went out and bought a couple of sandwiches, had lunch with her, and promised to return. As we were eating our supper, she suddenly said, "Wouldn't it be nice if Minnie could have a good, warm meal like we're having, instead of just a sandwich for lunch?" Rita jumped up, got some heavy-duty aluminum foil, fashioned a tray, and filled it with the food we had.

Little did we know at the time, that was the first loaf.

In the parable, when the disciples were faced with more than 4,000 people to feed and only seven loaves of bread and a few fish, Jesus asked them what they had to give. They gave the small amount of food—and their faith. To their utter amazement, they had abundant food for everyone. They had given what little they had, and they had trusted their faith. But they were an integral part of the miracle; *their concern, their love, their gifts, their faith* were the media through which the miracle occurred.

So Rita brought her one meal—and the miracle began.

She talked members of our small Christian Family Movement group into cooking meals—and the meals multiplied. She asked our fellow parishioners at St. Jerome's to participate—meals multiplied again. Rita was invited to speak to the Frankford Ministerium—more meals.

Pastor La Vonne Althouse, of Salem Lutheran Church, invited Rita to speak to her congregation at a special Mother's Day worship service. That was the beginning of a whole new ministry for Rita. She has since been to 106 Protestant and 100 Catholic churches delivering her message and recruiting volunteers.

Through one of the early volunteers, Aid For Friends was brought to the attention of Bernard Meltzer, the host of a popular Philadelphia radio talk show. He frequently had Rita on as a guest. Aid For Friends became his favorite charity, and he ran an annual fundraiser for many years before he left Philadelphia for New York. Many of Mr. Meltzer's listeners became regular contributors to Aid For Friends and still support the program. They formed the nucleus of Aid For Friends' financial base—yet another miracle of multiplication.

Back at St. Jerome's a trailer was donated to Father Lou Steingraber, and he invited Aid For Friends to have its office there. That office grew into three trailers on St. Jerome's parking lot and eventually into the double storefront office that we occupy in the shopping center directly across from St. Jerome's on Holme Avenue.

I could go on and on, but suffice it to say that today Rita's first meal has multiplied 3.5 million times. There are more than 7,500 active volunteers and 3,000 contributors, enabling Aid For Friends to serve more than 1,300 client-friends.

So many good things have happened over these past 19 years that I cannot help but believe in the strength of spirit and faith that have touched Rita and Aid For Friends. As miraculously as Aid For Friends has grown, so too has Rita grown. By taking one task at a time, by never running from a challenge, but relying on and trusting in her faith, she has become an extremely adroit administrator, a peerless motivator of volunteers, and a loving, caring person of immense depth.

I am happy—I am blessed—to have witnessed the miracle of Aid For Friends. As the disciples did, Rita brought her meals, her talents, her faith, her love, and her friends. They have been blessed and multiplied thousands of times over.

I trust that many of you who read *Faces on my Journey* will be touched—some will be deeply moved—and will in some way become a living part of a modern-day miracle.

Michael A. Schiavone, DDS
August 1993

Introduction

My understanding of success has changed radically as the Lord led me through life's journey these past 40 years.

I was a scholarship student from a blue-collar family, and Temple University offered me challenging opportunities. My academic degrees would bring social stature and professional employment—a far cry from the sweatshops in which my mother had worked at age 14. Of course, I would marry and perhaps interrupt my career for a family. The girl of 17 dreamed of an ocean-front vacation home, visiting countries throughout the world, and tasting other cultures. Who knew where success would lead me?

I had some ambivalent feelings, even then. Temple is in an inner-city neighborhood, and when I would see some poor soul dressed in tatters and obviously disoriented on Broad Street, I would think that perhaps, professionally, some day I might be able to help.

I became engaged, left school and married, deferring but not ending my education. I planned to work while my husband attended Temple University School of Dentistry. I didn't work very long, however, because two children were born while he was a student.

Our four sons were a joy (and continue to be as adults). I think parenthood can be the most joyful and at the same time most difficult of all vocations. It was especially difficult for me because after the birth of our fourth son, I was plunged into my first clinical depression. I was diagnosed as having a manic-depressive disorder, a condition that I have had to live and function with, often with great difficulty, these past 28 years.

Twenty-five years ago, Mike and I joined the Christian Family Movement (CFM) and with its "observe, judge, act," a life of actualizing Christianity opened new vistas and presented new challenges to me. I realized I had to reorder my priorities; swim club in the summer and ice skating club in the winter took too much of my time. I felt called to serve Our Lord by giving aid to His disadvantaged.

This was during the '60s when there was a great deal of consciousness raising and many people who had previously been very private people as Mike and I were became involved in an effort to help solve some of the community's problems. My husband and I did not think we had all of the answers, but we felt that we had to work to make the world a better place.

Our social milieu gradually changed. After Mike graduated from dental school, he set up a free clinic at St. Vincent's Orphanage for Children. He was the professional and volunteer and I stayed home caring for the children. But the CFM taught me that I, too, should actively work to help the disadvantaged.

CFM brought a succession of ministries. First, I was chairwoman for a Black-White dialogue in northeast Philadelphia. Then I volunteered for the Cardinal's Commission on Human Relations and developed various programs, the most enduring of which was the Community Food Distribution Centers program with 24 emergency food centers in the five-county archdiocese. I went downtown to the diocesan office four days a week and was home in time for my children to return from school.

When I left the Cardinal's Commission, I volunteered to help my Quaker friend, Marian Dockhorn, who was the director of the community office at the Frankford YWCA. She told me there were shut-ins who needed help. I visited them and found they all had two things in common: hunger and isolation. With free time on my hands, I began preparing extra dinners and delivering them to shut-ins. I didn't know it then, but these were the first of more than 3,250,000 free, frozen, home-cooked dinners delivered to shut-ins during the next 18 years. I developed Aid For Friends as an all-volunteer, nonprofit organization that provides free home-cooked dinners, friendly visiting, advocacy, and supplemental and emergency financial aid to the isolated disabled and frail elderly. I dreamed big dreams to help my fellow man and wasn't afraid of the challenge because I knew the Lord was always beside me.

Feeling better, after years of almost constant agitation or depression, I made appointments at both Temple University and Antioch College in Philadelphia toward the end of pursuing my goals in academia—but Aid For Friends was taking more and more of my time. My husband Mike and I made some decisions. I still had my responsibilities to the children and we thought I had to choose between being a volunteer or resuming my studies. Who would take my place at Aid For Friends? I chose my ministry to the shut-ins, with some sadness, still thinking I was deferring my dreams of academia until the children were out of high school.

Now, at age 58, I have to finally put my old dreams to rest. I have new dreams: to serve as many of the homebound as possible. We "feed the hungry, make welcome the stranger and visit the sick" (Matthew 24:35). To do this, I must constantly recruit volunteers. I speak after masses, at Protestant worship services, to service organizations, and to groups at synagogues. I try to motivate people to support our ministry and help it to grow.

Since 1974 we have enhanced the quality of life of thousands of people. Aid For Friends program currently serves 1,300 shut-ins in Philadelphia and its suburbs. Our main office is in a shopping center on Holme Avenue in northeast Philadelphia. Our network of volunteers consists of 7,500 people who cook, drive, visit, evaluate, coordinate, process our contributions and newsletter, and perform all of the tasks necessary to run our office. Twenty-five hundred others support our ministry financially. People also contribute through United Way Donor Option and additional support comes from Foundation grants. There are now three paid staff.

The Aid For Friends' shut-ins are no longer forgotten people, but important people. News of our work has spread. Through our program-planning manual, at least six groups in New Jersey, New York, and North Carolina have developed programs using Aid For Friends as a prototype.

My husband and I live a comfortable middle-class existence. He is my most treasured advisor and often takes time from his dental practice to support our ministry. With the grace and blessings of Our Lord, I plan to continue my work with Aid For Friends indefinitely. At times I still feel a dichotomy within me, but I don't have time to attend classes. Before I had problems with my vision, I could read late into the night; now that is not possible. Although I could go into business with 25 years of administrative experience and realize more of my girlhood dreams, my studies of Sacred Scripture and the teachings of Jesus leave me no alternative but to serve Him as He presents Himself to me in the scores of broken people who call for help.

Things seemed to be going relatively well until November 1990. I was scheduled for cataract surgery in January, having delayed it until I could barely see out of my right eye. Then, within five weeks, the problems started mounting. Mike was rushed to Wills Eye Hospital for surgery on both eyes for detached retinas. He was no sooner home than the emergency squad took Daddy to Nazareth Hospital. He had been having ministrokes and was becoming increasingly confused. Now he had suffered another stroke and a heart attack, and we weren't certain he would survive. Mom moved in with Mike and me, as we had previously planned, and arrangements were made to sell their home.

I had a mammogram and discovered that I had breast cancer. This took precedence over my cataracts and I had a lumpectomy, followed a week later by further breast surgery, radiation implants, and removal of 19 lymph nodes. With much sorrow, Mom placed Daddy in a nursing home, less than five minutes from our house, where he received constant nursing care. I tried my best to look after both of them. In late January, I started six weeks of radiation treatments.

I was devastated because I felt I had so many people to take care of, so many things to do, and I was so very weak. I prayed and told the Lord that if my strength was restored and I could take care of my responsibilities, I would work for Aid For Friends as long as I am able.

Gratefully, I have regained my strength and am able to continue my ministry. I am glad that my life can make a difference. Sometimes it is very difficult, but with Mike at my side, God always gets me through.

Since I founded Aids for Friends 18 years ago, I have been proud to volunteer my time. From the earliest, I was involved in every aspect of the program. Now, most of my time is spent administering a burgeoning organization, writing proposals, fundraising, and recruiting volunteers. As I said earlier, I developed Aids for Friends as an actualization of my faith in the Lord, feeling that it was my most important task, deferring pressing other needs.

In January of this year, I realized I could no longer ignore those needs. I must plan for my old age. At the insistance of the Board of Directors, I reluctantly decided to accept a salary. For 18 years, I haven't taken this step–I had to live my dreams–but now, at age 58, after much thought, discussion, and prayer, I came to the belief that I must continue to actualize the Lord's teaching's by serving the poor, sick, and hungry, but with this change. I have and will remain a volunteer cook, preparing and donating dinners weekly.

This year Aid For Friends celebrates its 18th anniversary. September marks a personal milestone for me as well: 25 years of community service. Sometimes, when I think of all the people who have touched my life—the poor, sick, hungry, and abused—my eyes fill with tears. Although my motive was to assist those who suffer from hunger, poverty, and suffering, t h e y have enriched m y life.

This book is about the faces on my journey these past 18 years: Dorothy, Freddy, Mary, Catherine, Marian, Cathy, and all of the others I have had the privilege of knowing since I founded Aid For

Friends. The isolated homebound clients and friends all tried their best to survive in an often harsh world. The helpers and volunteers I've included have inspired me with their unselfish dedication and sacrifices; they are extraordinarily compassionate.

All of their lives have touched mine and helped in the development of Aid For Friends. They have also left an imprint on my psyche. Their experiences served as a consciousness-raising tool that confirmed my conviction that I was to actualize my faith in God by dedicating my life and services to the isolated homebound. May God bless them all.

FACES
ON MY
JOURNEY
THE AID FOR FRIENDS STORY

I give you a new commandment:
Love one another;
Just as I have loved you,
You must also love one another.
By this love you have for one another,
Everyone will know that you are my disciples.

John 13: 34–36

Chapter 1
Minnie: Aid For Friends' First Meal

Marian Dorkhorn, the Director of the Community Office at the Frankford YWCA and a close friend of mine, told me about a Frankford area resident named Minnie. Marian was concerned because she was told that Minnie, who was handicapped and bedridden, had little to eat. My friend was very busy caring for the endless stream of visitors who came to her office seeking emergency nonperishable foods and other services. I volunteered to visit those who were unable to go to her office.

It was a hot, sunny day and Minnie's small rowhouse was suffocating. She sat on the side of the bed, her arthritic legs dangling and atrophied from disuse. The shades were down and it was dark, but Minnie didn't mind; in a very pleasant voice she explained that she had lost most of her sight.

The elderly woman introduced me to her daughter, Barbara, who stood unresponsive next to the wall. She seemed almost catatonic. Minnie explained that Barbara had been recently discharged from Friends Hospital. Barbara was a nurses' aide at Friends Hospital prior to her admission for psychiatric treatment.

Minnie was a sweet old lady, witty and intelligent. She didn't complain about anything and there was so much to complain about! Her bed linens and night clothing, although clean, were almost completely worn out. There was no fan to circulate the oppressive air. I walked to the kitchen to get her a glass of cold water and quickly discovered that there was literally no food in the house.

I was stunned by the urgency of the situation. I brought the water to Minnie, chatted with her, and inquired about her Supplemental Security Income and food stamp benefits. She wasn't receiving all she was entitled to and I told her that Marian at the YWCA's Community Office could probably straighten out this problem. She seemed pleased, and it was then that I asked her if she cared to join me for lunch. She pleasantly told me that she didn't want "to be a bother," but then acquiesced when I replied that there was nothing I'd rather do. After shopping at the corner store, I prepared sandwiches and cool iced tea, served them, and chatted some more. Then, with a kiss on her forehead, I told Minnie I'd be back the following day.

I left for home to prepare dinner for my family—one of my quickie Mexican dishes made with ground beef, onions, peppers, tomato, rice, and corn. As I served my children I told my husband about Minnie and her daughter and how much more enjoyable and nutritious the meal I had cooked for our family was compared to the sandwich I had served Minnie and Barbara. We also discussed the obvious fact that neither Minnie nor her daughter were able to cook. I immediately took out some tin foil and fashioned a tray to hold a portion of our meal to bring it to them the following day.

I called my friend Bernadette, a nurse, and we gathered some bed linens, towels, and a fan. We brought the articles along with my frozen Mexican dish. Bernadette bathed Minnie. We served the mother and daughter their dinner. I didn't know it then, but that was the birth of Aid For Friends.

Later I discussed Minnie's dire situation with Marian, who agreed to act as advocate and straighten out the disability benefits. Marian discussed other shut-ins she had been concerned about. I visited them to assess their needs. Help came from the YWCA, Frankford Ministerium, the Christian Family Movement, to which

I belonged, and the priests of my parish, St. Jerome. Members of St. Jerome's Community Life Commission became the first volunteers who promised to prepare and freeze dinners for the shut-ins.

On one of my visits I met Minnie's other daughter, Darlene. I didn't know quite what to make of her. She always seemed to be on a "high" and, instead of walking normally around the house, she took long, sweeping strides as though she was skating.

Darlene explained to me that her mother would need help only temporarily. Darlene's husband was due to be released from jail and she was enrolled in a methadone treatment program; she hoped that she would be over her drug addiction and back on her feet.

I helped them in every way that I could and really grew to love dear Minnie. I looked forward to my visits each week, but I was becoming increasingly busy handling all the referrals from social workers who had heard of our new program's services. I was visiting with and delivering meals to 11 shut-ins at the time and felt that Minnie's family needed a volunteer who could concentrate solely on their needs. Ceil, a member of my parish, offered to help and not only brought dinners, visited, and offered support, but shopped for them as well.

The following year an article in the Evening Bulletin resulted in contact with other churches and organizations and, through a new cook whose brother was a producer of Bernard Meltzer's Sunday morning radio show, financial aid. Mr. Meltzer graciously offered to tell the Aid For Friends story to his listeners and ask for support. We needed funds to purchase trays for the dinners and freezers to store the meals.

Darlene, true to her promise, recovered from her addiction. Within two years she returned to work and took over feeding and caring for her mother.

Minnie's story has been repeated continuously during the past 18 years. The names change and the nature of the disability varies but they all have one thing in common: they need help. The isolated homebound need nutritious, cooked food to eat. They need friends to talk to. They need to know someone cares.

A vision without a task is a dream;
A task without a vision is drudgery;
A vision and a task are the hope of the world.

Anonymous

Chapter 2

Dorothy

On a freezing winter day in 1974 that I shall never forget, I knocked on the door of a badly neglected house and met a woman who was to have a profound effect on my fledgling ministry.

A large woman in a tattered winter coat stood before me. Large safety pins held the coat together. The woman looked dirty and unkempt. Her nylon stockings were in tatters. As she bid me to enter the house, I noticed that it seemed just as cold as it was outside. My feet, clad in warmly lined boots, were tingling from the cold.

I told Dorothy about Aid For Friends services and that I heard she was sick. I then asked if I could start visiting her and bringing her our frozen dinners each week. She motioned me to sit down in "the dog's chair." Her little dog, Shotzy, was barking away, which made me nervous because I was frightened of dogs at the time. I tried to make the conversation as normal as possible. Suddenly Dorothy cried, "Do you feel the cold?" As I replied "Yes," she started sobbing. "I haven't had oil for two weeks...no food. I can't stand it any longer. I found rat poison and was going to take some and then give it to Shotzy."

I tried to reassure her and promised that I would have oil delivered by evening. Upset by Dorothy's outburst and plaintive cry for help, I desperately looked for the right words to calm her.

My legs felt like they were being bitten—I hadn't thought of the possibility of fleas—and I got up to leave. I didn't know where I would get the money to purchase fuel because Aid For Friends had no donors at the time, but I knew that I had to respond with immediate assistance.

Back at the Frankford YWCA Marian arranged to have the oil delivered through an emergency fund. I then took seven Aid For Friends dinners from the freezer and returned to Dorothy's. I had never seen anyone so hungry! She didn't want to wait for her first frozen meal to defrost.

Gradually Dorothy learned to trust and confide in me. The inside of her home looked like a haunted house with large cobwebs everywhere and old, musty, maroon draperies held together by safety pins; worst of all, a very bad odor permeated the entire house. I had been visiting the homes of poor shut-ins for five months and was accustomed to the sights and smells of the poor, sick men and women who were unable to care for themselves or their homes, but the odor that emanated from Dorothy's person was different from all the rest. (Later, when I took her for drives in my car, the terrible smell lingered long after I took her home.)

Dorothy slept on a broken down sofa, the base of which served as a home for a variety of mice. She said at night they would come out and crawl on her. The plumbing system hadn't worked for years; Dorothy used a commode that she simply dumped in the back yard.

She never washed because, I concluded, of an aversion to water. One day she panicked when I turned on the faucet in the kitchen. Dorothy knew I valued cleanliness and she tried to please me by dusting herself with Johnson's® baby powder. She thought the powder would give her a pleasant smell and cover up the dirty streaks on her arms and legs. The floor was filthy with the exception of large white spots where the powder fell. She let me cut her dirt-caked, inch-long nails. I bought her a fingernail brush and tried to explain that using it could keep her from getting sick. I also bought her some lipstick. She was happy with that.

The owner of the produce store on the avenue had been giving her his spoiled fruit and vegetables. When I saw them I was revolted and asked her never to go there again. Dorothy didn't have a refrigerator. On a shelf over the stove were a few eggs, an old, half-empty jar of mayonnaise, and a little container of bacon drippings that a neighbor replenished each week. (Small wonder Dorothy had chronic gastrointestinal problems.) The neighbor paid Dorothy fifty cents a week for carrying the trash cans to the back of her house. Dorothy always used a cane; she could barely walk! The neighbor probably thought she was magnanimous each time she gave Dorothy the money. I felt anger toward the neighbor and persuaded Dorothy to stop carrying the trash. I told Dorothy we'd see that she always had sufficient food, but she wanted the fifty cents to buy wine, and she asked me to go to the State Store to purchase it for her. She said she drank herself to sleep at night. It certainly didn't seem appropriate for me to supply her with wine but as our relationship developed I became less judgmental.

The old Native American saying, "Never judge a man unless you first walk two miles in his moccasins," was always in the back of my mind. How would I cope with mice running over me at night?

Dorothy's neighbors were disgusted with her because their street was a beautiful one except for Dorothy's property, which was overrun with weeds that covered the windows of the sunporch. I talked to one of the neighbors and found out they had always considered her "a little strange." Mrs. Smith told me that Dorothy's father had been concerned about his daughter's ability to cope with life once he and his wife were deceased.

I tried to change Dorothy's life. Volunteers attempted to clean the house. We paid for an exterminator with donations from St. Jerome's parishioners. Dorothy had no source of income but she hadn't always been poor: her father had been a railroad worker and a music teacher. A parishioner donated a refrigerator. I purchased new clothing from underwear to outerwear with money from a special collection at my parish. I couldn't get donated clothing in her size. She pretended that she washed it and always pointed out that the undies were drying on top of the radiator.

I know she was happy with her dress and yellow spring coat. She wore them proudly to a physician's appointment I arranged. After he examined Dorothy, the doctor took me aside and told me not to bring her back because her odor had fouled the air in the waiting room. "Take her to the hospital clinic," he said.

She refused to go. For some reason she thought "they" would commit her. I tried to reassure her otherwise but she was adamant. Dorothy was not psychotic. I had discussed her problems many times with my psychiatrist and he gave me useful insights and advice.

I remember conversing with Dorothy one morning when, out of the clear blue sky, she started sobbing. When I asked her what was wrong she told me how people in the community ridiculed her (supposedly behind her back) and made fun of her because of her appearance (for want of a better description, that of a bag lady). Her eyes filled with tears. As I kissed her on the forehead, and put my hands on her shoulders to reassure her, I thanked God that through His providence I was there that day. She desperately needed to feel loved. Although Dorothy had many positive attributes, she held herself in low esteem. In our interaction I always tried to raise her self-image.

Through it all, I was cramming books on social work, aging, and mental health. I prayed for guidance and perseverance. When the dirt and bad odors got to me, I said the Prayer of St. Francis meditating on his life. Always before me was the figure of the compassionate Jesus with the lepers and other castoffs of society, the Man for others, the personification of love. When situations were difficult to cope with, I'd tell myself, "Jesus never said it would be easy."

Gradually I came to understand that it wasn't right for me to try to persuade Dorothy to bathe, change, and wash her clothes. I subscribed to psychologist's Carl Roger's philosophy of "Unconditional Positive Regard." I had to accept her and love her the way she was—a child of God who had become a recluse, an eccentric with serious psychological problems, including an aversion to water, who could not cope—a 57-year-old who never matured into adulthood.

I brought Dorothy meals for three years, visited her weekly, and sold her large single house. I also reluctantly handled her money because she told me that if I didn't she would use it to "buy" friends the way she had used her father's insurance money....

A couple had befriended her after her father died. They moved in with her and she bought them a car. Dorothy showed me her bank book with the weekly withdrawals from her father's insurance policy. When all the money was gone they disappeared with the car, but not before tearing the house apart. They cut through the upholstered furniture looking for a cache of money they thought she might have hidden.

Dorothy was evicted from the first apartment I rented because of her odor, which spread through the adjoining apartments. The landlord was furious because the other tenants had threatened to leave unless she vacated her apartment immediately. Poor Dorothy was very upset. I put my arms around her to comfort her and kissed her on both cheeks. Tears streamed down her face. "No, no, Miss Rita, (I don't know why, but she insisted on calling me by that formal title) don't get too close to me. I saw people holding their noses. I don't want you to smell me. I know it's bad." I offered to give her a bath, thinking that then the landlord might let her stay, but she was unyielding in her refusal to bathe.

I frantically called real estate agents and finally found another apartment for rent. It was not as commodious, but I thought they'd take her. She was pleased that the apartment had a side porch.

One morning, I received a phone call from Katherine Polchek, one of our volunteers from a suburban county. She had driven to Philadelphia to deliver several warm nightgowns she had purchased for Dorothy and had planned to spend the morning visiting with her. Katherine sounded terribly upset as she explained that the police were taking Dorothy's body to the city morgue. Tears filled my eyes as she related the previous night's events....

The gentleman who lived in the apartment adjoining Dorothy's heard persistent knocking on his wall. He called her on the telephone and when there was no answer, he unsuccessfully tried to get into the apartment through the side door. When the knocking continued he called the rescue squad, who forced entry into the apartment. Dorothy was apparently experiencing a heart attack but she would not consent to go to the hospital with the paramedics. They tried to persuade her to at least permit a physician to examine her but she was too frightened to leave the security of her familiar surroundings. Reluctantly, the men left. When Katherine's constant knocking failed to rouse Dorothy, she became concerned and called the police. Dear Dorothy had died in her chair....

I made arrangements for a funeral service. My friend, Marian, who was the leader of the Southampton Friends Meeting, led the service. Eleven individuals from the neighborhood attended. Dorothy looked pretty in her powder blue gown.

The day after the funeral director prepared her body, he called and asked me if I had noticed her unusual odor. How could I not? He explained that the source was infected flesh. Dorothy never told me she had extensive open wounds covering her upper legs and lower abdomen. The funeral director said that it must have been very painful. My poor dear Dorothy! She never complained.

I knew I was fond of Dorothy but I didn't realize how attached I had become. The final separation from this special woman sent me into another severe depression.

I managed to go to her apartment the following month to dispose of her personal effects. I kept two items: her family bible and a photograph album. The photographs of Dorothy with her family were a revelation. She was obviously well cared for as a child, often photographed in a studio in the stilted poses of the Victorian era. There were also many shots of her family at the beach in Atlantic City, New Jersey. They seemed to be a warm, loving family enjoying their vacation. Dorothy looked precious in her little bathing suit. I gazed at the photograph of Dorothy's parents and wondered how shocked they would have been had they known their pretty child would become a recluse in rags.

When Dorothy died in her sleep... she wasn't hungry... she wasn't cold... she wasn't lonely... She was loved because of Aid

For Friends. I was grateful that our program enhanced the quality of her life during her last years.

There was $600 left in her bank account (I was the trustee), which I used to establish an emergency fund to help our poorest shut-ins.

Dorothy taught me something that became an almost subliminal part of our program: you cannot completely change a person or expect him or her to accept your values. Each individual must be free to live as he or she chooses and make his or her own value judgments. There must be choices available. We must always respect the dignity and integrity of each individual regardless of his or her living conditions. Most importantly, within each one of us there is a source of unlimited love, one of God's greatest gifts, and its little miracles turn strangers into friends.

Dorothy showed me that despite all of her problems she was sensitive to the needs of others. She demonstrated the true meaning of sharing: a dollar bill pressed into my hand ("buy something for yourself,"—I bought her candy), or an old salt shaker—even a daily prayer when one of my sons was ill.

I shall never forget the happiness that shone on Dorothy's face when Carol and I gave her a little birthday party. We sang "Happy Birthday" to her and presented her with gifts: a new dress, dusting powder, a cane. She laughed and clapped her hands, tears streaming down her face, while we lit the birthday candles, God's precious, precious child yearning to be loved and accepted.

I believe that she has now found peace, perfect love, and all the fullness thereof. Dorothy is with God and all the unreasonable fears, aversions, and phobias that haunted her have vanished. Her wounds are healed. She is like a rose in full bloom, its petals aromatic, soft, beckoning to be touched, held, admired. Our Lord has accepted her as others did not. I believe that although she may be in another time-space continuum, she knows how Aid For Friends has grown (at press time we currently serve 1,300 shut-ins), and I know she is happy about that. I'm certain we will meet again some day as we both walk in God's light.

THE GIFT OF LIFE

God's special gift
is no less beautiful
  when accompanied by illness or
weakness
    hunger or poverty
      mental or physical handicaps
      loneliness or old age.
Indeed, at these times
 human life gains extra splendor
  as it requires a special
   care,
    concern,
     reverence.
It is through the
 weakest of human vessels
  that God continues to reveal the
  POWER OF HIS LOVE.

Cardinal Terrence Cooke

Chapter 3
Mr. and Mrs. Smith

W hen I first founded Aid For Friends 18 years ago, I wondered why anyone as sick and disabled as John was wouldn't gladly go to a nursing home before the situation became urgent, but the thousands of shut-ins Aid For Friends has served since its inception have reinforced the lesson a homebound couple taught me in the first months of Aid For Friends.

Mr. Smith was handicapped and a paraplegic. He sat in a wheelchair clad only in a tee-shirt with a towel draped over his thighs. Mrs. Smith had cancer and other serious ailments; she was quite frail and in constant pain. They were very poor.

Since neither Mr. nor Mrs. Smith was able-bodied, their one-room apartment was in terrible shape: the floor was covered with trash and the sheet on the bed was nearly black with dirt. They had no support system. During the course of our initial conversation I naively mentioned a nursing home. The answer, delivered in strident tones by the gentleman, was "My wife and I were both employed in nursing homes all of our lives. We don't want to go there. We want our independence. I get up in the morning when I want to get up. I eat when I want to. I watch television when I want to watch it and I watch the shows I choose. I go to bed when I want to. In a nursing home, we will no longer make such decisions about our lives. We will be told what to do and when to do it. It isn't much, but this is *our* home."

Many individuals suffer tremendous losses as they age. They lose their mobility and cannot perform simple necessary tasks such as opening a window or replacing a lightbulb. Hearing and vision diminish, making communication more difficult. The elderly must cope with memory loss as well: they can't remember what they did five minutes before but remote and distant memories stay intact. The very old suffer social losses as their family and friends die. Unable to work, they also must deal with financial losses, especially women who lose pension incomes when their husbands die. Catastrophic illness exacerbates financial problems. This has created a class of people I call the newly poor.

These physical, social, financial, and cognitive losses are extraordinarily difficult to deal with and are major causes of depression for many seniors. Most of them, however, do not wish to suffer what is for them the greatest loss: loss of their independence.

Mr. and Mrs. Smith were not atypical in their resolve to maintain their home, however untidy it was. With an adequate support system many seniors can remain in the homes they treasure so dearly and live relatively comfortable lives.

I discussed the shut-ins' problems with Marian. After conferring with Mr. and Mrs. Smith it was decided that Marian would supervise a group of college students who enthusiastically cleaned the apartment from top to bottom. New sheets were bought for the bed and my friend secured additional help.

Mr. and Mrs. Smith took pride in their newly refurbished apartment. They deserved the best we could give them.

This only is charity,
to do all we can.

John Donne

Chapter 4
Helena

Another person I remember fondly was Helena. Dear Helena, who became ecstatic at our first meeting because she recognized my voice from the *Bernard Meltzer Show* and had never met anyone "in person" who had been on the radio. She had surgery for a brain tumor that, along with a host of other ailments, had left her with severely limited mobility. She was usually in good spirits and had a good deal of faith.

Her visitors were wonderfully supportive. They not only brought the meals, but also performed the many household tasks she was no longer able to do.

I called her one day and she seemed unusually excited. She made a will and was leaving her little house to Aid For Friends. I didn't know what to say. She said Aid For Friends had "given her so much hope." I told her she mustn't feel she should pay us back, but she seemed to get such a thrill that she too was going to give to Aid For Friends and help other shut-ins. On my next visit she gave me one of the afghans she made before her illness. Helena was a prolific crocheter and there were many afghans draped over the chairs and sofa. I admired her handiwork and told her I would treasure it.

She slipped into psychosis shortly after that and became

delusional. Poor Helena thought the man next door came through the wall every night and raped her. Within six months of her initial psychosis she died.

Her attorney called me and explained that the money from the sale of Helena's home must first satisfy her debts and nothing would be realized by her bequest to Aid For Friends. That did not in any way negate her generosity.

Thinking about clients and friends who have died is no longer depressing because they are still a part of me and our shared experiences taught me many things and helped me grow as a person; they helped give meaning to my life. I believe life on earth is fleeting and those who have left are walking with God in His light. His graciousness and His love for His children is unconditional, boundless, and eternal.

Life's most persistent and
urgent question is:
What are you doing for others?

Martin Luther King, Jr.

Chapter 5

Cathy and Mr. Burton: A Neglected Parent

Mr. Burton was constantly anxious. He had many serious problems: prostate cancer, heart disease, emphysema, cataracts, and crippling arthritis. He was a victim of parent abuse, had little money, and was chronically depressed. Mr. Burton also had the distinction of being one of Aid For Friends' most difficult clients and friends. In just one year's time three visitor volunteers left because they simply couldn't cope with him.

I came to the conclusion that he had special needs and required a special visitor. One of my best friends, Cathy Pfeiffer, was the answer to my prayers. Mr. Burton would have been impossible to care for if Cathy, who volunteered as the fledgling program's director of operations as well as a visitor, hadn't been blessed with the patience of a saint.

Mr. Burton's two alcoholic daughters, Agnes and Wilma, were verbally and at times physically abusive to their father. He was often bruised from his daughters' rough treatment but would not let Cathy report his daughters to the authorities. Both daughters neglected him and unfortunately, as do many adult children, they didn't wish to assume responsibility for the care of their parent. Agnes said she was "too busy and didn't have the time." Wilma told me the sick gentleman was "able to care for himself if he really wanted to."

It is my personal belief that the elderly person who struggles to raise a child and later finds himself or herself virtually abandoned when there is nothing left to give that child suffers more than the individual who never had a family. In 18 years of serving the homebound elderly, I believe this is the most common cause for situational depression in isolated, frail, elderly parents.

Although I originally founded Aid For Friends to provide assistance to the isolated homebound who have no family, I quickly had to amend the eligibility requirements to include the homebound who had children who were unable or unwilling to provide their parents with adequate nutrition and the necessary support services. Mr. Burton was obviously in this category. His two daughters took turns shopping for him weekly and thought that small effort fulfilled their responsibility to their parent.

All of these factors caused Mr. Burton to be overcome with anticipatory anxiety: the "what ifs." "What if Cathy doesn't come this week with my dinners? What if she doesn't take me to my doctor on time? What if the doctor doesn't have my test results? What if the social worker can't get another homemaker to help me?" (Mr. Burton wasn't able to keep a homemaker longer than a few months because he was so difficult to deal with.)

Mr. Burton's method of handling these anxieties was to verbally abuse Cathy and telephone all of his caregivers (Cathy, his physician, and social worker), at least once a day. If he wasn't satisfied with a given caretaker's response to a call, he telephoned that caregiver every hour. All except Cathy lost their patience and one by one terminated their services to Mr. Burton. Cathy tried to explain to him that his behavior was often the cause of the interpersonal problems complicating his life, but he would not, or could not, change.

Cathy was very busy raising her three young children and I counseled her in setting limits to cope with Mr. Burton's persistent calling. The young mother was doing her best to deal with his problems because she understood how sick, lonely, and frightened the poor man was. She told Mr. Burton not to call her more than once a day unless there was an emergency. She always called before her weekly visit to see if he had any special requests. Cathy explained that she had to care for her family and could not give him all of the time and support he demanded from her but, if he cooperated, she would make certain that his basic needs were addressed. That was a tall order but she was true to her promise.

Sometimes Cathy brought her children to visit Mr. Burton and his attitude always changed. He was pleasant and obviously enjoyed chatting with the young ones. He told them stories and entertained them with little tricks.

He would often shout expletives at Cathy, however, because of his anger about his physician's inattention. She would struggle to maintain her composure, calmly tell Mr. Burton that she couldn't tolerate such behavior, and leave. She would no sooner arrive home than Mr. Burton would be on the telephone to apologize for his behavior and thank her for her support. My friend's inherent goodness and faith enabled her to persevere despite his cantankerous outbursts because she recognized in him a pleasant gentleman who was driven to desperation by fear.

Through Cathy's ministrations his two daughters, Agnes and Wilma, became more supportive and stopped their abusive behavior. This never would have happened without my friend's intervention and constant attention to Mr. Burton's needs.

The elderly man often talked about ending his life by slashing his wrists. Individuals who threaten suicide are frequently dismissed as attention-getters, but talk of suicide is a frustrated, desperate cry for help, and depressed individuals often carry out their threats.

The elderly man was often the proverbial "pain in the neck." Mr. Burton was rarely pleased: when Cathy brought his dinners, which were carefully selected because he liked only chicken and turkey dishes, they were sometimes criticized vociferously. Gifts of clothing were always the wrong color. He disliked me because he thought I didn't care about him, although I did empathize with him. I was always apprised of his problems and discussed possible solutions to those problems with Cathy.

Cathy always forgave his outbursts and served him faithfully through the years. She saw the good in Mr. Burton and respected him. This compassionate woman had actualized her love for God by serving His suffering and forgotten in the best way she knew how. May God bless Cathy for her neverending kindness.

The causes of parent abuse are many: children are under the influence of alcohol and other drugs, are tired and stressed out from their parents' demands, or just have little patience and bad tempers. Many adult children have problems in their own families and, unfortunately, lash out at the most helpless—a sick, elderly parent.

The solution to this problem is not simple, but adult children should remember that their frail elderly parents are as helpless and dependent as children and worthy of all the time and patience they can muster. We must not treat the elderly like children, however, but treat them with dignity and try to respect their wishes. It is a privilege to serve them. Counseling in cases of parent abuse is often helpful. If not, it is best for frail elderly parents to be removed from dangerous home situations. Very often they will not press charges out of fear, loyalty, and love.

Charity is never lost:
  It may meet with ingratitude,
  yet it ever does a
  work of beauty and grace
  upon the heart of the giver.

Conyers Middleton

Chapter 6
Nora and her Friends

Nora was a woman with young children when she volunteered as both cook and visitor volunteer for Aid For Friends. She visited an elderly couple in a third floor apartment and an 84-year-old woman.

Nora was the only visitor Elizabeth and Joe had. They were so disabled they couldn't leave their apartment, even to go to their physician. Elizabeth was bedridden and incontinent but she had a sense of humor. The poor woman had an allergic reaction to disposable diapers and was able to wear only cloth ones. Nora provided personal care to Elizabeth and did the elderly couple's laundry each week, including Elizabeth's diapers. The shut-ins knew that Nora's children were all boys and used to joke with Nora, "Did you ever think your baby girl would be this big?"

Edna, the 84-year-old woman, was very frail and had congestive heart failure and arthritis. She was a pretty woman with a very sweet disposition. In addition to visiting Edna, Nora provided personal care to her as well.

One day before Edna died, she told Nora that she always made certain to tip everyone who provided any service to her or did her any favors. "Except for you, Nora, I don't ever tip you." Nora replied that no one would ever tip a daughter. "No, no," she replied,

"I wouldn't tip you because you're an angel. You were sent to me by the Lord. You are a gift. You can't pay angels." Nora wrote to me that no one will ever say anything to her that will affect her more. Nora, her husband, and their sons treated these three elderly folks as family (would that all children show their parents such love and compassion).

Nora and her family prepared many of the dinners for their "family" themselves, sometimes as many as 50 at a time. Her husband and sons also visited Edna, Joe, and Elizabeth. The elderly couple loved to tell stories to the youngsters and often would get out old photograph albums.

Nora told me she believed that Elizabeth, Joe, Edna, and all of the needy who come to us are the Lord saying to us, "Here I am. Love me, feed me." The last years of Elizabeth, Joe, and Edna could have been filled with loneliness, hunger, and misery. Nora and her family gave them a taste of our Creator's love and compassion. Now that they are in heaven, they enjoy the fullness of God's unconditional love.

Stewardship is what
a man does after he
says,
"I believe."

W.H. Gruver

Chapter 7

Franny and her Children

One day a young woman accompanied by three small children walked into the office of the Frankford YWCA and asked for food. It was an insufferably hot day and the poor little tykes, although clad only in sunsuits, were worn out from walking in the blazing sun. Marian Dockhorn introduced me to the family and suggested I drive them home with their package of groceries. The children were precious and reminded me of my boys when they were younger.

Marian talked to me about Franny when I returned. I had not yet focused on the isolated homebound as a requirement of eligibility for Food For Friends' meals. My friend suggested that I give frozen dinners to Franny's malnourished children.

Marian always impressed me as the perfect social worker: nonjudgmental, respectful toward her clients, calmly seeking solutions to their problems. She indicated that Franny needed a support system and urged me to look in on them weekly and offer help wherever appropriate.

Franny had a reputation in the neighborhood as being promiscuous. I wasn't trained to deal with family problems, but Marian promised me she would guide me.

I visited Franny, Tommy, Kate, and little Frankie every week.

The kids really tugged at my heartstrings and I would bring along little games for us to play with. They were used to canned food and the homecooked Aid For Friends frozen dinners were a real treat for them. Their appetite improved and they gained weight.

I brought cleaning supplies because Franny couldn't afford them and she spruced up the house. Franny seemed happy with the changes in her life and I felt she was earnestly trying to be a good mother and homemaker.

Then during one of my visits, the divorcée confided in me that she thought she was pregnant and had decided to keep the baby and love it. I knew that she was looked upon as being promiscuous, but during previous conversations she revealed that she yearned to meet the right man and have a two-parent family for her children. She thought that her boyfriend might marry her someday. I wondered if it was wishful thinking. I didn't believe I had the right to dictate her lifestyle, but I good-naturedly suggested that, although I was happy she was going to keep the baby, it would be better if she try not to get pregnant again until she was sure she married "Mr. Right," who would be both a good husband and father. Thankfully, to her surprise, the pregnancy turned out to be a false alarm.

One day Franny was waiting at the door when I arrived. She excitedly told me that little Frankie was sitting on the ledge of a second floor window, slipped, and fell onto the pavement below. The doctors at the hospital examined the little boy and, unbelievably, found no injuries. Frankie's guardian angel certainly seemed to be working overtime: he was playing as usual and seemed unaware that the accident could have been fatal.

Months passed and all three children seemed to be thriving, but one morning I received a call from Marian. The mother and her children disappeared. I was almost in tears as Marian explained that the neighbors dealt with Franny in their own way. I drove down to her whitewashed house and parked the car. There before me someone had painted in black letters three feet high WHORE. My heart ached for Franny and her children. I really didn't think she was a prostitute. I made inquiries but couldn't get any leads as to her whereabouts.

One day I received a phone call from Franny and she told me she rented a house in another neighborhood about one half hour away. I immediately brought some of the Aid For Friends frozen dinners, games, and clothing for the children. We were overjoyed to see each other. The kids hugged me tightly as I swung them around to their gleeful cries. They loved to hug me and sit on my lap. The children were constantly infected with head lice, which both the school nurse and Franny treated. I hoped that I wouldn't bring the lice home to my children.

I had learned to tolerate the sights and smells of the needy, but I couldn't get comfortable during my visits to Franny's and was always glad when the time came to leave because the place was overrun with roaches: on the floor, on the walls, and on the ceiling. Every so often one would drop down on the floor or table. I literally prayed that none would fall on my head. It was really a shame because the ubiquitous insects seemed to ruin all efforts to make the run-down house livable. Franny was distressed by the roaches as well but a major exterminating job was way beyond her financial capabilities.

One day, I drove down Franny's little street for my weekly visit and noticed that the white curtains I bought her were gone from the windows. I rushed to the door and rang the bell repeatedly, afraid there would be no answer. I made inquiries to no avail. I never saw Franny or her three precious children again.

Franny wanted the best for her children. I believe that a strong support system could have helped her cope with heading a single-parent family. She had no parents herself or role-models to guide her. Many young women with children trapped in the cycle of poverty desperately reach out for love and security, but their desperation often clouds their judgment. I didn't have any solutions. There were no special programs to help pull Franny's family up from the morass they were in. I pray that somehow Franny was able to offer her children the security they needed and that the youngsters grew to adulthood untraumatized by the events of their early years. I will never know.

We are all so much
together and yet we are
dying of loneliness.

Albert Schweitzer

Chapter 8
Help for Jack

J ack lived in the Port Richmond area and had chronic heart failure. He was in and out of the hospital constantly. Jack's efficiency apartment was very bare: a bed, a wooden chair, and a refrigerator. Sample cases were stacked against the wall, memories from the days the elderly gentleman had been a traveling salesman. There was a single lightbulb hanging from the ceiling. Initially, we had no visitor for him, but because he needed help so urgently, Cathy, Alicia, and Joe delivered meals to him. Finally, after several months, we were able to get a visitor.

When Frank went to Jack's apartment he discovered that Jack had just been released from the hospital. The room was very cold because there was only a space heater. Jack was still in his hospital gown and he had no blanket; his feet were purple. There were no clean clothes. The generous visitor stayed with Jack for a while, gathered up all the clothing, went home and washed them, and brought them back to Jack along with a new blanket from Aid For Friends.

Cathy talked to Jack's social worker because the landlord obviously exploited Jack (he paid $200 monthly for this horrible room), but the social worker said that if any complaints were made, the landlord would throw Jack out. She tried unsuccessfully to get him into a boarding home. We were worried about our meals because Jack's refrigerator was broken. Providentially, Frank, our volunteer, was a repairman and fixed the refrigerator.

He delivered the dinners weekly and supported Jack in every way possible. Jack died last year, but because of Aid For Friends volunteers he knew that he was cared for and loved.

There was a man, a mystic, deep in prayer
to the One God. As he prayed, there passed
before him the lame, the hungry, the blind,
and the neglected and seeing them, he became distressed and cried out in anguish.
"Oh, Creator, how can You be a loving God
and yet do nothing about helping these
suffering people?"
There was no sound as the holy man waited,
and then a voice pierced the silence, "I have
done something about them…I made you."

A Sufi teaching story

Chapter 9
Millie's Sacrifice

As the result of a holiday radio fundraiser by Bernard Meltzer on WCAU, a woman named Millie from an upstate county in Pennsylvania began sending an annual check in a plain envelope for $1,000–$2,000 in 1980. I was so excited! I concluded that such a generous gift must be from someone who was relatively affluent.

When the woman didn't give one year, I assumed she had gone to our Lord. The following year, however, a check came in January. I called Millie on the telephone to personally thank her and ask how she was feeling. She was so sweet and ingenuous. Millie apologized for not giving the previous year and explained that she had been laid off from her factory job. She then proceeded to explain how she was able to accumulate savings for charitable donations.

During the winter, Millie collected firewood to burn in the basement of her home. She and her sister lived in the cellar during the cold weather, which precluded the necessity for any central heat throughout the house. She rode her bicycle to the factory every day. All fuel and transportation savings were used to support her church and serve the Lord's suffering and hungry people at Aid For Friends. But then the modern day St. Francis paused and said, "I don't know if I can do it any longer. I'm getting old and the cold bothers my arthritis so. I'll also be retiring from my job soon."

I listened quietly in disbelief and awe at the sacrifice this benefactor had made. We chatted for awhile and I asked if she ever came to Philadelphia because I would love her to see the organization that she and her sister had helped build over the years. I then added, "Please, now that you are older and your arthritis is bothering you, move back upstairs and let other people support the Aid For Friends ministry financially. You were the first person to donate $1,000 to Aid For Friends and are in a very real way part of God's plan to build this program to take care of His sick, hungry, and lonely. Rest on your laurels and now offer your prayers for our ministry in a warm home."

That was two years ago. I haven't heard from her since, but I'm certain her prayers are with our shut-ins.

Commit everything you
do to the Lord;
trust Him to help you do
it and He will.

Psalm 37:5

Chapter 10
Mary's Little Miracle

Neighbors found Mary lying unconscious on the sidewalk and they called the rescue squad. At the hospital the doctors diagnosed the cause of her collapse as malnutrition and severe hypertension. She also had crippling arthritis and suffered from anxiety and depression. Mary was referred to us by a neighbor and I called immediately upon her release from the hospital.

Mary ushered me into a room that was piled high with cartons. She was obviously a "collector," one who cannot bear to part with a lifetime of memorabilia and therefore accumulates everything. Mary's hands shook and her eyes filled with tears as she motioned to me to sit down. She looked much younger than her age, almost childlike: a clear, unwrinkled face and not a gray hair amidst her short, dark brown hair.

I explained the program to her and told her that a special visitor volunteer would be assigned to visit her weekly for an hour and deliver seven home-cooked frozen dinners to her. She started shouting and crying, "It's a miracle, It's a miracle!" I was perplexed by her outburst and wondered if she was delusional until she explained that she had been praying to the Blessed Mother for help because she was so desperate. Aid For Friends was the answer to her prayers—a miracle!

Mary loved the dinners; spaghetti and meatballs was her favorite dish. A friend of mine, Jerry Leimkuhler, who had been an Army nurse during World War II, became her visitor. She was very kind and supportive. Each week she brought a bag of fresh fruit and cinnamon buns from the local bakery in addition to our dinners. Jerry also took her to the bank each month to cash her disability check.

I was in constant contact with Jerry because she was our contributions coordinator and came to my house every week to work on the records. She often talked about Mary's depression and encouraged me to go along with her on her weekly visits, thinking I might be able to help Mary and offer her insights because I had been in psychotherapy for many years. I no longer wanted to become personally involved with our client/friends, however, because I had been devastated by Dorothy's death and had suffered another clinical depression. In 1979 Aid For Friends was expanding and I had to concentrate all of my energies on caring for my family and carrying out my duties as volunteer administrator.

Then Jerry unexpectedly brought Mary to my house one afternoon. Company! I was upset because I was severely depressed at the time and in constant psychic pain just forcing myself to perform the tasks that were necessary for Aid For Friends to function. Interacting with others caused even more pain. At that time, I was struggling to survive.

Mary seemed to be a nervous wreck as she talked about the half-hour trip to my home. I tried to empathize with her fears and managed to get through the visit.

Within a year Jerry became too ill to drive and visit. I was no longer in a depressed state and felt that I was the natural choice to replace her because Mary was not afraid of me.

Mary was suspicious of just about everyone; she thought people were out to take advantage of her. Finally, she started to trust me and realize that I would never do anything to hurt her. I wanted her to know that I had her best interests at heart. It took some persuasion, but she finally let me arrange for a gentleman to come from Social Security to arrange for her benefits. She was not receiving all she was entitled to because she mistrusted all strangers.

One morning while Mary was going up the stairs she experienced one of her frequent dizzy spells. The frail woman was holding a glass of orange juice. She fell down the steps and landed on the container. The shards of the juice glass severed an artery in her wrist.

Although she was in shock, she managed to crawl to the phone and call a neighbor who immediately called the emergency squad. By the time Mary arrived at the hospital she was in critical condition due to blood loss. She gave my name as next of kin and they called and said Mary was asking for me. My husband, Mike, took me to Frankford Hospital immediately and I nervously braved the confines of the elevator to see my friend. I was very phobic at the time and terrified of many things, the elevators and long corridors of the hospital among them. But my love for my friend and prayers gave me the courage to visit her. Mary recovered and went home in a new lilac housedress I bought for her.

I was shocked to find that as soon as Mary was out of the hospital, she returned to the weekly job she had struggled to keep in order to pay her medical and home repair bills. Mary was exploited by the proprietor, who paid her just two dollars an hour to clean his luncheonette. She paid for the cleaning supplies out of her meager salary. I implored her to quit because she was sick so often. She suffered constant pain and dizzy spells and she could hardly stand. Mary would come home from work on Sunday afternoon and collapse for three days because of the strain. Despite her determination to be self-reliant, the poor woman finally did quit because it was no longer possible to push herself beyond her physical limits.

Mary lived frugally with her thermostat set low at 62°. The house was not well insulated and the cold and drafts exacerbated her arthritic pain. When she quit her job, I told her Aid For Friends would be able to help with emergency repairs and arranged for students from De LaSalle Vocational School to weatherize her home through a collaborative effort.

Mary and the Psychiatrist

I felt I wasn't making any headway with Mary because she continued to cry during part of every visit and each time I called her on the telephone. I talked to her about my own history of depression and explained how helpful and supportive a psychiatrist could be. After months of gentle prodding, she finally consented to start psychotherapy on one condition: I had to be present at all times. I was not thrilled at the prospect of being part of a process that I knew from my own experience could be emotionally draining, but I had no choice if I really wanted to improve Mary's quality of life. I reluctantly decided to give her the support she had requested and made arrangements to take her to Dr. Bachman for the first time. He was not only a skilled practitioner, but a kind and gentle man who managed to gain her trust almost immediately. Although Mary always became upset when she got ready for her appointments and often felt sick to her stomach on the ride to the doctors, she calmed down in Dr. Bachman's presence. Little by little her story unfolded...

Mary entered the convent after high school, but within the year, her father brought her home to work in a factory. There were hard times and the family needed the extra income. She had led an active life and played tennis regularly. An excellent swimmer, she taught classes at the neighborhood youth center. The athletic young woman must have been self-confident and outgoing.

Mary married in her late twenties. Her family had never liked her husband, who was a bit of a lady's man. The young woman had always dreamed of a large family, but her husband was adamant in his refusal to father any children. He eventually moved in with his girlfriend.

Mary apparently became so depressed that she stopped eating altogether and was hospitalized for dehydration and malnutrition. Later that year her family conspired to drop her off at Philadelphia General Hospital after telling Mary they were taking her to the hairdresser. Mary cried as she related how two men then put her in a strait-jacket and took her away to the state hospital. There she was terrified and attempted suicide with a bed spring. The tiny woman felt that all of the other patients posed a threat and she constantly prayed for deliverance. The chaplain befriended her and, realizing she was not psychotic, arranged her release. For the rest of her life Mary was convinced that her family had conspired to put her in the mental hospital to get rid of her and gain control of her house.

Dr. Bachman managed to allay her greatest fear: she was never crazy, would never become crazy, and no one could ever put her in a mental hospital again. Gradually, a breakthrough came and she stopped crying every time she spoke. The doctor prescribed a low dose of antianxiety and antidepressive medication that proved to be most helpful.

Nicole and Mary

Mary's first visit to my home proved to be a very special day for me because my Aid For Friends' "friend" showed an emotion that in five years of contact I had never observed before: joy— unequivocal happiness—unadulterated by the various aches, pains, and miseries she had suffered for so long. Not that they ceased to exist—no big miracles here—just little miracles that love can bring. The instrument of this respite was not myself (although I believe my unconditional love for Mary brought her comfort and raised her self-esteem) but Nicole, my vivacious, charming, and beloved granddaughter.

We spent about an hour and a half at my home together and, after the initial warming up period, Nicole sensed Mary's gentleness and ingenuousness. They played peek-a-boo, hide and seek, and other little games together and Nicole, like almost all two-year-olds, talked and giggled and screeched happily in an absolutely delightful way. Mary laughed as I have never seen her do and the two of them communicated their love, their faces radiating excitement and happiness.

Mary talked about Jerry Leimkuhler, her former visitor volunteer who was no longer able to visit because of poor health, and about the Aid For Friends frozen dinners and the soups she often eats for lunch. They have helped her immeasurably.

It was the holiday season and I measured the hem for a new dress for her and gave her a poinsettia. There was also a bag of personal care items with some cookies and candies on the top.

As if on cue, the postman brought to the door a box of hand-knit slippers from one of our supporters in Cape May, New Jersey. I gave some to Mary because she wears them all day and they keep her feet warm at night.

My little story of the happiness and loving that children can bring is but one of many engendered by Aid For Friends. Many of our younger visitors take their children with them when they visit shut-ins. Isolated individuals hunger for loving attention; Aid For Friends meals and visits fill a great, dark void in their lives.

A Christmas Visit

During Christmas week 1986 my family piled into my son's van for a visit to Mary. I had a feeling of déjà vu as I recalled how my four young sons used to pile into our station wagon with my husband, Mike, at the wheel when I served with the Cardinal's Commission on Human Relations in the late '60s to bring food, clothing, furniture, and gifts to inner city families. Twenty years later my son, Joe, was at the wheel with his wife, Ann, and daughter, Nicole, at his side. Mike and I squeezed into the back and we went off to Olney. Mary loves Nicole; she longs for the children she never had.

Nicole, who had been animated and full of Christmas spirit in the van, became very quiet when we entered Mary's house. The shut-in, of course, was no stranger to the child, but Nicole had never been in a house quite like Mary's before. She stared wide-eyed at the cluttered surroundings: there was just a path that led from the living room through the dining room into the kitchen. Broken television sets, lamps, boxes of books, linens, broken dolls, and other memorabilia were piled up.

We gave Mary the Aid For Friends presents donated by our

supporters and some personal ones as well. With shaking hands she started unwrapping the packages. She loved the warm flannel pajamas and robe. There was also a lovely pink sweater and seven pairs of handknit slipper socks. I presented my friend with a large poinsettia for her front window. She liked her neighbors to know that she had friends who brought her gifts. The plant gave her a sense of pride.

Mary cried with happiness. On cue, Nicole gave her some dusting powder. The visit was going well, but I wished Nicole would warm up to Mary; however, she just sat quietly by my side. I tried to engage her in Christmas conversation with the elderly woman to no avail. We stayed for about an hour as Mary tried on the gifts. She was happy that I brought my family along for the Christmas visit, but was obviously disappointed that Nicole did not respond to her entreaties to play.

After our visit, as we walked up the street to the van, Nicole grabbed my hand. "Grandma," she said plaintively, "Mary is very sick isn't she?"

"Yes, honey," I replied.

Then she continued, "Mary is very poor isn't she?" I didn't know what the term "poor" meant to Nicole, but replied again in the affirmative. Then—I shall never forget this—Nicole announced to me in a firm voice, "Grandma, somebody should take care of her!" I reassured Nicole that Aid For Friends and I were trying to take care of Mary's needs.

Nicole was only four years old at the time, but she had the wisdom and the intuition to recognize suffering and poverty, to recognize not only need but also responsibility.

Compassion clothes the soul with the robe
of God and divinely adorns it. And those
who follow compassion find life for
themselves, justice for their neighbors,
and glory for God.

Meister Eckhart

Chapter 11
Mrs. Jones and Son: Hungry and Cold

The winter I first heard about Mrs. Jones and her son they were two tragic figures desparate for food.

Mrs. Jones, who was in her 90s and very sick with cancer, weighed just 62 pounds. Her son, who was in his 60s, was very ill as well. When Mrs. Jones returned from hospitalization following surgery, she found neither heat nor water in her home because the pipes had frozen. There was no food.

It took the city five days to correct the situation and both she and her son were greatly affected by the extreme cold. The frigid air inside the house affected Mrs. Jones' tongue so that she could barely speak. She and her son were starving. In desperation, she called her doctor and asked for help.

The dedicated physician called a convent that was close by asking if it was possible for a nun to bring food to two of his patients. When Sister received the call from the doctor she immediately brought his patients dinners from one of Aid For Friends' freezers, which is located in the adjoining church. When she went to their home she found the stove and oven inoperative.

Sister put through a call to our office and then immediately went there to pick up a toaster oven for the couple. We had no visitor volunteers available, but Sister told us not to worry because she would gladly volunteer her services until a permanent visitor could be found.

Mrs. Jones and her son have been receiving help for more than five years now and I am most grateful that we were able to help mother and son get through that crisis. But the good news is that five years later they are doing so much better.

Cathy and I visited the little family last summer and Mrs. Jones was a delight! She proudly showed us all of the plants that she grows on her sun porch, including beautiful orchids she has cultivated for many years. Previously Mrs. Jones raised annuals in her back yard and sold the flowers from a stand in front of her home, which provided a supplement to her meager social security payments.

Mrs. Jones then took us into her living room. I admired the intricate carving on the original Victorian furniture that she and her husband purchased when they first married. Everything in the room was a bit faded but, despite her age, she still managed to keep a neat and orderly home.

During the holidays, Mrs. Jones' wonderful visitor brought her to our open house. The 95-year-old woman is a feisty lady who has a twinkle in her eye and a marvelous sense of humor. I gave her a big hug.

You may call God love, you may call God goodness, but the best name for God is compassion. God prompts service among brothers and sisters. In that way, one creature sustains another. One enriches another and that is why all creatures are interdependent.

Meister Eckhart

Chapter 12
Little Miracles
Love Can Bring

W hen I first visited Sally to evaluate her needs, the smell of animal feces and urine was almost overwhelming. The dog, Sasha, and eight assorted cats left droppings throughout the house. These animals were Sally's reason for living. They were her family.

Born with cerebral palsy, Sally had always been confined to a wheelchair. She received no support services from the government and lived a desolate existence in the first floor of the little house her parents had left her.

I was very wary of Sasha because her upper lip was curled and she kept growling at me. Therefore, I stood just inside the door—there was really no place to sit except a mohair sofa that was thick with years of dust—and told Sally about the Aid For Friends free services, describing some of our meals. I hoped she would consent to become part of our program because she obviously needed assistance. It was chilly because the shut-in always kept the side window open for her cats. I was thankful that at least some fresh air came into the house. I took mental notes as I evaluated Sally's living conditions and listened to her life story. I realized that the middle-aged woman was probably inured to the foul odor because she lived with it every day. The environment was unhealthy, however, and I thought that once she met her visitor, who had to be very special, perhaps Sally might ask for help in cleaning the place.

The next day another little Aid For Friends miracle took place. Peg, the mother of eight children, volunteered as a visitor and "adopted" Sally. Because the shut-in had been confined to the first floor of the house for many years, she didn't have access to a bathtub or shower. To Sally's delight, Peg took her home, where there was a bathroom on the first floor, and gave her a shampoo and shower. Sally said it felt "heavenly." The trip became a weekly ritual. At Sally's request Peg tackled the years of dirt that had built up in her home. Then, every week when Peg delivered the Aid For Friends dinners and visited with Sally, she cleaned the house as well. Sally, who was a shy and very sweet woman, eventually told her new friend she wished she had some new furniture. Providentially, Peg's next door neighbor had just ordered new furniture and was only too glad to give her still serviceable living room and kitchen set to the shut-in.

Sasha was still a problem, however. The dog had long hair that reached the floor and literally mopped it all day long; Sasha was filthy, but everyone was a little frightened of her—except Sally, of course. One of my best friends, Annamae Carroll, has a special way with dogs because they sense her great love for all living things; she's a modern day St. Francis. When I asked Annamae for help she immediately went to Sally's home, made friends with Sasha, and trimmed and bathed the dog.

Sally was so happy with her new life. She loved Peg's family, who had accepted her as one of their own. The shut-in took pride in her home and enjoyed the dinners; the good nutrition had improved her general health. I was grateful to God for another Aid For Friends success story. Food and friendship: little miracles love can bring.

Only a life lived for others is a life worthwhile.

Albert Einstein

Chapter 13
A Horror Story From the Past

Mrs. Rosen had called *The Bernard Meltzer Show* asking for help. He had been conducting a Holiday Fund Raising Drive for Aid For Friends. Mrs. Rosen didn't fit the profile of our usual referrals in that she wasn't homebound, but she sounded so disturbed and troubled when I called that I made arrangements to drive to her home the next day.

On our first visit, Mrs. Rosen nervously invited me into her kitchen for tea and freshly baked coffee cake. Her face seemed frozen into a mask of suffering. Bits and pieces of her tale unfolded. She told me of her flight from the Gestapo, of how a Catholic family had hidden her in their barn in Czechoslovakia, and how she left on a quest for freedom but was captured and sent to a concentration camp. I do not know when she married. I listened, offered my compassion, but did not invade her privacy by asking questions.

She stopped her story abruptly and asked me to leave. The following week, Mrs. Rosen called me and again invited me over for tea. At that time she introduced me to her husband, who looked extremely depressed, and then took me on a tour of her well-kept home. She proudly showed me the houseplants that were placed on sills and shelves throughout her home. She had a "green thumb" and had many varieties, most of which she grew from shoots. She selected a large, attractive one and offered it to me as a gift. I treasured it because I knew how much it meant to her. We then spent two hours sharing a pot of tea as she revealed more of her past. She had suffered horribly as a result of being hunted and brutally imprisoned during World War II.

I visited her six or seven times. With each visit I was struck by the depth of her anxiety and anguish, which must have been as acute as the fear she had experienced 30 years before. As Mrs. Rosen shared her past experiences with me and talked about her current problems, I realized that the past was mixed up with the present and she was not able to differentiate the horror of her incarceration during the war from the present reality of her freedom.

One day she confided that she was saving "evidence" to use against the "doctors." Mrs. Rosen pointed to a row of medicine bottles filled with pills on her kitchen window sill. She excitedly told me that they had been prescribed by her doctor for various ailments but that the bottles, in fact, all contained poison—a conspiracy between the doctor and her pharmacist.

Mr. and Mrs. Rosen had many physical problems as well. She had chronic gastrointestinal problems because the victims in Auschwitz were permitted time for bathroom functions only once a day. He suffered from prostate problems. Mrs. Rosen was distraught over her husband's chronic depression. He could not speak without crying.

The poor woman and her husband obviously needed general medical attention and, I believed, a psychiatric evaluation. I became determined to act as their advocate. One day, I asked if she would like me to ask a doctor, who was a friend of mine, to look in on them. She agreed and arrangements were made for the two of us to visit that weekend. The visit did not go well. Mr. and Mrs. Rosen had been conditioned not to trust—and hope had died in the concentration camp. The doctor thought they both needed psychiatric care before their physical problems could be addressed.

I called an acquaintance at the area mental health center in the hopes of obtaining help for the couple. Unbelievably he told me, "Frankly, I'd rather not accept that woman as a patient because she'll be too difficult to deal with." After my emotional plea, however, he did arrange an appointment for a psychiatric evaluation. When I explained to Mrs. Rosen that she might feel better if I took her to a mental health center to see a doctor about her depression, she adamantly refused to go. The poor woman became very upset and explained to me that all doctors were members of the Gestapo.

I didn't know where else to turn. I called several Jewish agencies but couldn't get any leads. I thought that a rabbi might reason with her, but she refused to go with me to the synagogue. She told me she had called several rabbis before and they were no help. That she was paranoid there was no doubt: she told me of the neighbors' "plots" against her.

The following week I received a pair of handknit brown gloves in the mail with a note. Mrs. Rosen hoped the gloves would match my coat, but in the note she told me not to come or call again. Crestfallen, I called her immediately but she told me not to contact her at their home because the presence of strangers was too upsetting to her husband. From now on, she declared, she would come to visit me and clean my house. I was in a quandary because I didn't want Mrs. Rosen to think that yet another person had let her down, but I certainly didn't want her to become my housekeeper. Second, upon consultation with my psychiatrist, I decided I could not cope with the problems that would arise if she had constant access to my home.

Mr. and Mrs. Rosen were not part of the Aid For Friends' shut-in feeding program, which was expanding and required more and more of my time. At the same time I had four young children at home to care for and had to deal with my own serious, chronic, emotional problems. I felt powerless to give the elderly couple the help they needed. Sadly, I realized I could not be all things to all people and that no matter how hard I tried or how good my intentions were, I could not make a positive change in everyone's life.

I knew that my relationship with Mrs. Rosen would have to

have limits, or I would become so burned out that I wouldn't be able to help anyone. Although many years have passed, I still think of the couple in sadness and wish I could have taken their terrible years of suffering away. Mrs. Rosen wanted me to provide her with a support system that I was incapable of giving, but despite that, I still feel that I failed her.

Now I read so much about concentration camp survivors' organizations; however, at that time I couldn't find any support group for her, though I doubt she would have participated. Mr. and Mrs. Rosen are two victims who survived Auschwitz, but in bearing the horror they were mentally wounded for life. I tried communicating with them several more times but had to respect their wishes and ceased contact. I could not ease their pain. I pray they have finally found peace.

Each of us has within us a
Mother Teresa and a Hitler.
It is up to us to choose what
we want to be.

Elizabeth Kübler-Ross

Chapter 14
Mrs. Williams

During a reading at one of our Interfaith Services, I thought about one of our neediest client/friends, Mrs. Williams. The reading was from the great prophet Isaiah and dealt with the kind of day that is pleasing to the Lord.

"...to share your bread with the hungry...clothe the man you see to be naked... If you give your bread to the hungry and relief to the oppressed, your light will shine in the darkness...."

Give relief to Mrs. Williams, I thought. I was worried about her and she was never far from my thoughts. Let me share her story.

Janelle and I walked up the front steps. I noted that the house and surrounding garden were obviously well maintained and wondered how the son, who lived with the elderly woman we had come to see, could assume responsibility for the maintenance of his mother's home and concurrently abuse her.

We rang the bell, and through the window I saw a slight figure in the kitchen—her movement was so slow it was almost imperceptible. We waited, and then slowly the door opened. Mrs. Williams beckoned us in as she painstakingly positioned her walker in front of the sofa and slowly sat down. She was quite frail and emaciated; her worn clothing hung from her lanky frame. I worried about her tripping because the soles of her shoes were wound with masking tape and the tips hung loosely. Mrs. Williams sat quietly and waited for us to speak.

To break the ice I asked Mrs. Williams how she was feeling and her sad story unfolded. Showing me her knobbed, twisted hands, she told me she had suffered from arthritis for 30 years. As a result, she had extreme difficulty sleeping because of the excruciating pain. Mrs. Williams was also recovering from a recent hip fracture, had rapidly failing vision, and underwent frequent hospitalization.

"My phone was disconnected because my son didn't use my Social Security check to pay the bills. He uses it for himself. Could you look for my electric bill? I can barely see, no longer able to read. I am afraid they are going to cut off the electricity. When I ask my son a question about paying the bills, he gets very angry and takes it out on me. I am afraid of him and may ask him to leave." She asked me to call her social worker, who was a wonderful young woman from a senior center working diligently to set Mrs. Williams' affairs in order.

I explained the Aid For Friends operation to Mrs. Williams and asked if we might send a weekly visitor to her and bring her meals. She responded that she thought that was a good idea, and I then asked her if she might have difficulty heating her frozen dinners in the oven. I wondered, in view of her incapacity, if a toaster oven would be less difficult. Her brow furrowed as she replied that she thought a toaster oven would help because she couldn't possibly stoop to use the oven, but she couldn't afford one. I told her not to worry and that a volunteer would bring her meals and a toaster oven within the week.

As we got up to leave, I talked about the Chanukah/Christmas project and asked if there was anything special she would like for the holidays, suggesting an article of clothing. As we stood there, she thought for a moment, started to speak, hesitated, and in a very small voice replied, "I guess I could use a pair of shoes and a sweater." Getting the reply I had hoped for, I told her we would make arrangements immediately and, with a gentle touch to her shoulder, Janelle and I departed.

Mrs. Williams was the third case of parent abuse referred to Aid For Friends that year. The agencies were trying to work out solutions to some of the problems. Mrs. Williams was in a bind because she wasn't quite capable of living alone but she didn't want institutionalization. There were no available visitors, so I called her former pastor, Reverend Burns, for help and suggested a team of visitors because of her son's instability. The pastor's wife and another member of the congregation volunteered to deliver the meals and visit. The church even offered to pay for the toaster oven.

Mrs. Williams quite obviously needed the nutritious meals and a caring relationship. Her life had been so difficult, frustrating, painful, and heartbreaking for so many years, we had to try to reverse the momentum and introduce something positive into her life: trust, hope, love.

Mrs. Williams enjoyed the meals and was comforted by her visitor volunteer. Her social worker arranged for a van to bring her to the senior center three days a week, where she was served lunch, interacted with other seniors, and participated in group activities.

Although we all implored Mrs. Williams to evict her son, she could not bring herself to take that final step. The elderly woman was terrified of him and may have been fearful of retribution. However, she had given this child life, raised him, and lived with him. Perhaps she simply loved him as only a mother can love a child and was afraid of losing her only son. She did not share her deepest feelings, but kept them locked inside her heart.

The only way in life to endure man's inhumanity to man is to try in one's own life to exemplify man's humanity to man.

Alan Paton

Chapter 15
Freddy: A Hero

Kevin and I had gone to see Freddy because his visitor of five years had been hospitalized and could no longer volunteer. When we arrived, Freddy was eating—a task that was exceedingly difficult for him. A green plastic trash bag was tied around his neck as a bib. (We take so much for granted).

Freddy, age 51, is a handsome man. He was born with cerebral palsy and is profoundly disabled with very poor motor control. He has a severe speech impediment and must make a great effort to communicate his thoughts and feelings. It is quite apparent that Freddy is very intelligent, practical, courageous. He accepts his problems with equanimity and is determined to live outside a protective environment in the mainstream of life.

Freddy asked us to come to his home because he wanted to show us something. He talked of his low SSI payments (for the poor disabled), his need to be economical, and the high cost of heating oil. He took us on a tour of his sparsely furnished three rooms, pointing out areas where the cold air was coming in and suggesting solutions. He asked if we could get a volunteer handyman to do some insulating and repair as soon as possible. He was very worried about the winter months. Aid For Friends had helped him with problems in the past and we told him that we would make every effort to give him the assistance he requested.

His friend John, who at that time shared the apartment with him, came in. John is also severely disabled by cerebral palsy, but is able to walk with difficulty. He painstakingly started making the bed and straightening the room.

As Kevin carried in a donated television and radio, we talked about the recent robbery of Freddy's apartment. He was terribly distressed by the incident. The thieves had ransacked the little apartment and stolen not only the television, radio, and clock but, unbelievably, the battery pack from Freddy's electric wheelchair.

Freddy and I often talked on the telephone. Sometimes he would say he had just come back from work. I didn't want to seem too inquisitive, but I couldn't conceive of any task Freddy was capable of performing for a salary. His speech was barely intelligible. It was necessary for an aide to come each morning to provide personal care. One day my curiosity got the best of me and I asked Freddy where he worked. This is his story.....

Each morning after his nurse's aide cleaned, bathed, and dressed him, Freddy started his arduous journey. First, he drove his motorized wheelchair down the ramp and onto the street, traveling several blocks until he arrived at the trolley stop. After patiently waiting for the trolley car that went to the subway, he would steer his wheelchair onto the tracks. The motorman had no choice but to stop. Many of them were used to Freddy and didn't mind taking both him and his wheelchair onto the trolley car. Some, however, got angry.

At the end of the line, Freddy always managed to persuade some strong passerby to help him get onto the subway platform. He would then travel to Center City, get off at 13th Street, persuade someone to bring him to street level, and then slowly drive his wheelchair to a large Center City Catholic church frequented by many workers and shoppers in the area.

Freddy sat at the church entrance with an old hat at his feet most of the day. Some of the worshippers placed coins in his hat. Freddy was a familiar figure to many of them and the most compassionate always had a kind word for this brave gentleman.

The reason this daily journey was necessary was because Freddy didn't receive sufficient disability funds to pay his nurse's aide and he couldn't survive outside an institution without daily support services. He had thought his problems and challenges through when he chose to leave the home for the disabled.

Freddy's plan for survival worked well for many years. Then, unbelievably, a social worker took action to reduce his state aid. Miss Adams observed Freddy's "work" and reported his additional income to the authorities. She was an atypical social worker; most members of the helping profession are extraordinary human beings. Consequently, the poor gentleman's assistance was reduced. To make up for the deficit, Freddy found a boarder, John, whom he met at a gathering for the disabled.

I always felt intense respect and admiration for Freddy. When he was through telling his tale, I wished that our conversation hadn't taken place over the telephone because I wanted to reach out and give my friend a big hug. Such courage!

To the passerby along the busy street in front of the church, Freddy's appearance may have seemed that of a beggar, and that he was. He was reduced to begging in order to live as close to a normal life as he could within the confines of his disability. That is why Freddy became an advocate for the disabled in Washington, D.C. He understood that increased government assistance would not only allow an individual to have the option of independent living, but the cost to the state would actually be less than institutionalization.

Very often we read in the newspapers about individuals who have done something heroic or who have performed a service to the community. In the conference room at the Aid For Friends office there is an assortment of awards we have received over the years for our work with the poor, hungry, and sick. Do you know who should really be recognized? The Freddies of this world who, despite almost insurmountable handicaps, struggle with perseverance and ingenuity to cope with their world. They deserve the highest accolade. They don't want a plaque or a certificate honoring their achievements, however; they want and deserve help in the ways that t h e y think are best. In my eyes, Freddy is a first-class hero!

Freddy's Surprise: The Dance

One day, Freddy called me and excitedly told me he had a surprise. Although Freddy's mind works quickly, he must struggle to enunciate the words and articulate his thoughts. He was very patient with me as, bit by bit, I picked out a word or two I could understand until I finally got the entire message.

Freddy's voice was tight with emotion as he told me he was going to get married. His fiancee was also profoundly disabled with cerebral palsy. My friend asked if she would be eligible to receive our meals and I immediately said, "Of course." He was so happy!

In Isaiah 49 Yahweh says, "Before you were conceived in the womb, I knew you...I shall never forget you...See, your name is written in the palm of my hand." That means my name, your name, and Freddy's and his fiancee's. Our creator has always loved all of us unconditionally and will do so for all eternity.

As children of God, what is our responsibility to our brothers and sisters? I do not know why Freddy and Julia had the misfortune to be brain damaged at birth and cannot walk or speak clearly. Life on this earth is fleeting when measured against eternity. I believe that in another dimension Freddy and Julia will be free of this life's genetic, physical, and psychological makeup and environmental and social conditions and, with God, they will run and dance and sing and accomplish all the things they dream of. For now, however, I can work and speak on their behalf and serve them because of God's love for me, Freddy, and his fiancee and my love for them.

I shall never forget Freddy and Julia's wedding day wheelchair dance. It was the most moving dance I have ever seen and the most unforgettable wedding reception I have ever attended. Freddy was the beaming, proud husband and gracious host in his black and white checkered formal jacket. Julia was the shy bride, so happy, so excited.

Julia wore a long white dress, and there was a short veil pinned to her hair. She was strapped in her wheelchair because the cerebral palsy made it almost impossible for her to control her movements. They were elated and their happiness was contagious. As I congratulated her, I was not able to understand her response, but Freddy did and that is all that matters. Happiness is having someone to love and receiving love in return.

One of Freddy's friends belonged to a combo and they played at the reception. As they played the first few bars of "I'm Getting Married in the Morning," Freddy and Julia positioned their wheelchairs opposite one another. He grasped her right hand with his left and, using their feet and with some difficulty, they pushed against the floor, rocking their wheelchairs back and forth. They didn't miss a beat. They were very excited and obviously greatly enjoying their dance together.

Freddy's and Julia's dream was the same as those not afflicted with a disability: to live in their own home sharing their lives together, good times and bad, pain and joy. I did not know how they were going to cope, but Freddy was resourceful and determined (in other circumstances, he would have made an excellent attorney); I knew that the Aid For Friends program would help them live out their dream and for this I was most grateful.

Freddy's Thank You

Freddy was the featured speaker at Aid For Friends' Tenth Anniversary Interfaith Service and Celebration. He spoke very slowly and, with extraordinary effort, thanked the volunteers and contributors for their help. Then he said that God works through all of us and what a wonderful tribute it is to God to be there. Freddy was most impressive. His depth of faith is humbling. Once you come to know him or others who have similar handicaps, you look beyond the disability and realize it is merely physical because their spirit is free, strong, healthy, limitless, and substantial. In many ways, they are not handicapped at all.

Freddy was eloquent. I believe he is gifted with a superior intellect. So often people will see an individual handicapped by cerebral palsy, severe motor problems, and extreme difficulty in speaking and assume that he or she is mentally handicapped as well.

Freddy is aware that it is difficult to understand him. He spoke slowly and explained that he "belonged" to Aid For Friends for five years, that he liked the meals very much and they helped him a great deal, and that they were now helping his wife, Julia. But to him, Aid For Friends is much more than that. It brings friendship. It reminds him of Jesus' words to the disciples, "Whenever you do this to the least of these my brothers, you have done it unto me." He talked about God and said we are our brothers' keepers and ended by thanking us. He then asked the congregation to "help Rita to help more shut-ins." There we sat, not a dry eye in the church, all of us working and sacrificing for the Aid For Friends ministry, but Freddy's gift to us that day was priceless. It was indeed a privilege to know him and to help him live as he chose: independently.

INVICTUS

Out of the night that covers me,
Black as the Pit from pole to pole,
I thank whatever gods may be
For my unconquerable soul.

In the fell clutch of circumstance,
I have not winced nor cried aloud;
Under the bludgeonings of chance
My head is bloody, but unbowed.

It matters not how strait the gate,
How charged with punishments the
scroll,
I am the master of my fate;
I am the captain of my soul.

William Ernest Henley

Chapter 16
Ted and Eileen: Two Lifesavers

I was talking to Ted one day and he said, "I thank God for giving me the health and strength to visit Anna. I can't see why everyone isn't a visitor volunteer. It makes me feel good to know that because of my efforts, someone else's life is so much better." Ted told me that Anna really enjoys the Aid For Friends dinners and soup he brings and added that he brings her crackers and a variety of fresh fruit each week because she has no other source of food.

Anna is in her mid-50s. She is below average in intelligence but was able to work in a factory for many years. Anna is now legally blind and suffers from arthritic pain. She looks forward to Ted's visits and he is the only person she talks to all week. Anna receives just $230 per month in disability payments and of that sum, $140 must go toward the rent for a single basement room. The room has no cross ventilation and the heat is oppressive during the summer and fall. During the winter months the room is very, very cold because the heating system in the house does not function properly. The only furnishings are a bed, chair, small refrigerator, and hot plate. There is no phone.

Anna rents the room from her aunt, who grudgingly lets her stay there and often threatens to put Anna out. The aunt ignores Anna's needs completely and there is contact between them only rarely. Last December, our holiday gifts for Anna included a warm fleece jogging suit and a blanket that were donated by Aid For Friends' generous contributors.

Ted heard me speak at his church eight years ago and despite the fact that he holds two jobs, he has been a volunteer visitor ever since. (The first shut-in he visited was a terminally ill woman in her 50s who, despite the fact that she had raised 10 children, received no support whatsoever from her daughters and sons. Ted was so good to her during her last years of life). Ted thanked me for opening new vistas for him. I could not thank him enough for using his love, compassion and empathy—gifts from God—to effect changes in other people's lives.

Leo is in his late seventies and has diabetes, severe crippling arthritis, and uncontrollable high blood pressure, which causes constant dizziness. Leo worked in an office until he became disabled. He lives alone: his wife died 10 years ago. They had no children.

Leo's brothers and sisters have exploited him and bled him dry during these past 10 years. They have taken items from his small home and tricked him into signing over the deed to his seashore retreat. He is confounded by such cruelty and suffers from a "broken heart." Sometimes he is very bitter and responds to his visitor's kindness with suspicion. He is in a constant state of depression.

Eileen, his visitor volunteer, has been a light in the shut-in's life: faithful, dependable, supportive, cheerful. She visited him almost daily while he was hospitalized because she understood how fearful he was.

Leo loves the meals! Whenever I talk to him, he goes on and on describing each day's dinner to me. (He had been hospitalized for malnutrition before he was referred to our program.) Sometimes he tells me that Aid For Friends is the only reason he is still alive. In addition to the meals and visits, we have helped him in several financial emergencies. He asks how he could ever repay the volunteers for all they have done for him. I tell him that the help is from strangers, with the exception of Eileen and myself, who want to share and show their love, but he insists he must do something. I tell him, "Leo, just remember all the Aid For Friends helpers in your prayers."

While I was reading Scripture one day, Ted and Eileen were on my mind. In the Beatitudes our Lord tells us, "Blessed are those who hunger and thirst for what is right for they shall be satisfied. Blessed are the merciful for they shall obtain mercy." In First Corinthians, I read, "Love is always patient and kind, it is always ready to excuse, to trust, to hope...love does not come to an end." To me, these verses describe Eileen, a young woman just out of college, and Ted, a man in his 40s. I thank God for Aid For Friends because were it not for our program, they would not have met Anna and Leo and the shut-ins' cries would have gone unheard.

These two shut-ins occasionally see family members, but the pain of loneliness is piercing their very souls because they suffer psychological abuse. They are two people exploited, literally crying in the night. Now Anna and Leo have food to eat and friends to share their pain with. Their dark days have some sunlight in them because they know that despite all their physical and mental suffering they are loved.

Eileen and Ted have made a conscious choice to reach out to the hungry and the sick—and they are richer for having known these special children of God. The Lord must indeed smile on them.

Lord, teach me to be generous.
Teach me to serve You as
You deserve;
to give and not to count the cost;
to fight and not to heed the wounds;
to toil and not to seek rest;
to labor and not to ask for reward —
save that knowing
that I am doing Your will.

Ignatian Offering

Chapter 17
Mother and Son

A concerned ambulance driver called our office to ask about assistance for a woman he had just taken home from the hospital. Although this driver is confronted with poverty and suffering daily, the Magee family's circumstances seemed to him to cry out for help in a special way.

Mary Kay, our outreach worker, immediately visited them. The mother, who wore leg braces for her crippling arthritis, was senile and deaf. The son, who was in his 40s, was mentally retarded.

Mary Kay and I went back the next day to further assess the situation. The refrigerator and stove were broken beyond repair and the television and lamps were inoperative. There was no electricity throughout most of the house. The sofa's covering was worn down to bare foam rubber that had yellowed with age.

The son smiled, at first uncomprehendingly, as we tried to explain Aid For Friends services and asked for permission to help them. As I rubbed the mother's cold, arthritic hands to warm them, her son told me that with great difficulty, he had been traveling once a day with his mother to a coffee shop in Frankford. The daily coffee and doughnuts were their only sustenance.

Mary Kay visited them each day and mobilized agency resources for nursing care. I found a new visitor volunteer who had experience: a Catholic nun, a social worker, who would visit each week on her day off.

At times Mrs. Magee was in touch with reality, but quite often she spoke of two of her children and her deceased husband as though they still lived there. After observing the interaction between this mother and her son for a period of two weeks, Mary Kay, Sister Joanne, and I arrived at the same conclusion: although Mrs. Magee and her son lived in unbelievable circumstances, there was obviously a great deal of love, affection, caring, and support in their little family and we should marshal the resources necessary to help them to continue living together.

First we purchased a toaster oven and a supplemental package of nonperishable foods. Then we obtained a small refrigerator freezer to hold Aid For Friends frozen meals. We bought a floral throw cover to brighten the sofa. For the future, we hoped to acquire a hearing aid for Mrs. Magee.

When I went home that day I felt neither depressed nor overwhelmed as I often do when confronted with exceptionally severe cases. I felt hopeful and elated as I thanked God for all of Aid For Friends volunteers and supporters who made possible the continuation of the simple life for this mother and son in their little home. Judging from photographs on the wall, the house, which was where the son was born, had known better times and once contained shiny paint, bright wallpaper, and new furniture. The house could not ever have known greater love, however, than the love these two trusting creatures of God had for one another.

When one reaches out to
help another,
he touches the face of God.

Walt Whitman

Chapter 18
The Amazing Buddy

Every once in a while I come across a shut-in whose attitude, despite great misfortune, is absolutely amazing. Buddy tops the list because not only was he not bitter, but he spread his positive philosophy of life to everyone with whom he came in contact.

He became permanently disabled when he was 42 years old. Buddy was referred to us when he was 64 after being discharged from the hospital where he had been treated almost continuously for nine and a half years. The shut-in had suffered seven strokes and three heart attacks. He was also diabetic, asthmatic, and blind in one eye. He had several tumors and suffered frequent dizzy spells from Meniere's disease.

Buddy said he didn't have time to think about his illnesses because he was too busy working on his physiotherapy and exercising in hopes of regaining his lost mobility. He spoke about Aid For Friends and how at first he didn't think he could survive outside an institution. Buddy found out, however, that our program not only made his independence possible but that, surprisingly, it also helped make his life a pleasure.

The gentleman spoke about his visitor, Nan, with much affection. Nothing was too much trouble for her. Each week before she visited him and delivered her frozen dinners, she stopped at the store and picked up any items he needed. The shut-in said she was "superlative, dedicated, and had a sparkling personality." Nan brought the outside world to Buddy and chatted with him about life, news events, and her family, and he no longer felt isolated. Her husband, George, was a regular "Mr. Fix-it." Buddy had been worried because he didn't have the money to replace his broken electric razor and he was too disabled to use the conventional type, but George had the razor humming within a week's time. He fixed other appliances for Buddy and helped keep his little home in tip-top shape.

Buddy had great faith and spent an hour of every day in meditation, never forgetting to thank God for the gift of each day spent without severe pain.

The shut-in taught by his example that there can be joy in living for all those who have faith in themselves. He told me one day that he was "glorious because I am maintaining my independence and how grateful I am to have achieved this level of self-sufficiency."

For Buddy, each day brought new challenges and he used them to learn how to make succeeding days easier to cope with. The gentleman told me, "Tomorrow I will do better and be better for what I have accomplished." Buddy could have justifiably felt sorry for himself, but if he had done so he would have lived his days in unhappiness and actually would have been more disabled. Instead, he chose to "thank God for small blessings" and made the best of a bad situation. He was not only amazing, he was a wise and great man.

To a brave heart nothing is impossible.

French Proverb

Chapter 19
Theresa's Journey Ends: November 1984

Theresa's journey on earth has ended. Aid For Friends was part of that journey for 10 years. When I was the sole visitor in the early days of the program, I took her some of her first meals. As the program grew, Toni and Martha became her visitors and steadfastly looked after her for nine years.

Toni called me one evening to explain that she had called the emergency squad. Theresa asked Toni to accompany her to the hospital, which Toni did. The physician in the emergency room said that Theresa suffered a massive heart attack. She quickly lapsed into a coma after the attack.

Toni anxiously called me and explained that Theresa had often expressed concern about having a "decent funeral." She had no family and no will. Over the years, she frugally saved $1300 from her meager SSI payments. Theresa died the day after the heart attack and I spent several hours with the hospital's director of social services, representatives from Temple University Law School, Judicare, and the funeral parlor. I made arrangements for her burial and hoped that I wasn't doing anything illegal.

I remember the afternoon I first met Theresa. She was a little difficult to communicate with at first because she had a speech impediment. She moved about slowly with the aid of a walker. I was always nervous when I visited her because an unfriendly dog lived next door.

Toni and Martha volunteered in response to an article in *The Evening Bulletin*. They visited Theresa and four other shut-ins. The volunteers found it difficult to interact with her because her verbal responses were always flat. In addition to her disabilities as a result of a stroke, she also had psychiatric problems, which were serious at times. In fact, she was often paranoid. Theresa, because of her background and emotional problems, was not a trusting person and Toni and Martha, who were so generous and caring, found that difficult to deal with. We had a meeting and they decided that they would continue visiting her in view of the circumstances.

Theresa and her brother were born in Cleveland, Ohio. Their parents left them in the first of many unhappy foster homes and moved to Australia. Theresa married in her teens. Her husband, acting as her pimp, drugged her, prostituted her, and beat her often. After three years, she managed to leave him and move to North Philadelphia where she rented a room to live in and worked in a factory. In her 40s she suffered a stroke that left her too disabled to be gainfully employed. She applied for welfare and moved to a small apartment in a housing project. She didn't attend church and never talked about religion, but there was a large picture of the Sacred Heart of Jesus on her table.

Toni and Martha helped her find an apartment in a better housing project. They also did banking and chores for her, took her to doctors' appointments and shopping, etc. Another volunteer, John, also took her on errands. She loved the meals and when I look back I feel good about the part Aid For Friends played in her life. She had good nutrition and the care and concern of Aid For Friends volunteers who certainly had enhanced the quality of her life.

Toni and Martha took her to a nearby park when the weather was nice. Once they took her to Atlantic City. Theresa was very excited about the trip.

I am grateful that Aid For Friends made her last 10 years on this earth so much better. Toni and Martha epitomize what Aid For

Friends' visitor volunteers can be. As for me, I shall remember Theresa as I last saw her when the volunteers brought her to the Aid For Friends Interfaith Service at Holmesburg United Methodist Church. She looked so much better than when I had first visited her. Her hair was curled, she wore a new red and white dress, and she had a smile on her face.

Now all of her pain, both physical and mental, is gone forever and her tragic life is just past history. I believe there is a healing of memories and she is with her Creator, walking without the aid of a walker in God's light, enveloped by His unconditional love in another time-space continuum for all eternity. Perhaps I shall see her again some day.

Lord, make me an instrument of
Thy peace,
Where there is hatred,
let me sow love,
Where there is injury, pardon,
Where there is doubt, faith,
Where there is darkness, light,
Where there is sadness, joy.
O Divine Master, grant that I may
not so much seek to be consoled as to
console; to be understood as to
understand; to be loved as to love;
for it is in giving that we receive; it is
in pardoning that we are pardoned;
and it is in dying that we are born to
eternal life.

Prayer of St. Francis of Assisi

One of my favorite prayers was written 800 years ago by a
man who serves as a role model for many of us. St. Francis of
Assisi denied himself the wealth and comfort of his family
and, because of his religious convictions, chose to beg for the
poor and serve the sick.

Chapter 20
Dr. Frankl's Self-Transcendence and Mr. Walton

One of my favorite authors is Dr. Viktor F. Frankl. He is an Austrian psychiatrist who developed logotherapy and is the author of the classic, *Man's Search for Meaning*, which details Dr. Frankl's search for meaning while he was incarcerated for two and a half years in Auschwitz and three other death camps during World War II. During his imprisonment he counseled other prisoners and gave them a "why" to live. (Friedrich Nietzsche: "He who has a *why* to live can bear with almost any *how*.")

I was rereading the notes I had taken about Dr. Frankl's article when the mailman came and I received a letter from Mr. Walton that related exactly to Dr. Frankl's concepts of self-transcendence. The letter was one of the most touching I have ever read. I had met Mr. Walton six months earlier at an interview and information session for potential visitors. As I read the beautifully written four-page letter, I was filled with awe at the resilience of the human spirit.

Mr. Walton was born with a facial disfigurement and a speech impediment. Because of this he suffered rejection in his childhood, adolescence, and adulthood. The middle-aged man was also born with the gifts of intelligence, empathy, and a remarkable, trusting faith in God. Through all of his trials and tribulations—and they are too numerous and too personal to recount here—he never lost his faith but remained resolutely determined to give meaning to his life. He could have felt sorry for himself, a victim of man's inhumanity to man. He could have believed that life owed him something because of the cruel treatment he received from so many individuals throughout his life. Against all odds, however, he maintained faith and hope and is an admirable, compassionate person who offers himself and his talents to others. He serves as a paradigm for all of us.

Frankl believes that the "defiant tower of the human spirit" balances on two foundations: an individual's twin capacities for self-transcendence and self-detachment. Self-detachment is the ability to detach oneself from things outside of oneself, to put distance between them, or to confront them. An example of self-detachment is when one sublimates his own needs and wants for the benefit of others or for his religious beliefs (eg, prisoners in concentration camps courageously helping one another).

Just after the World War II, Frankl began using the nomenclature "self-transcendence" for the ability of an individual to rise above and beyond oneself and commit oneself, in love, to the service of others. In Frankl's logotherapy he counsels that an individual's reason for existence should not be hedonistic, the pursuit of pleasure and wealth, the gratification of his own needs and wants in this consumer-oriented society. Instead, the *raison d'être*, the justification for existence, should be the preservation and elevation of human values and human dignity. Theology tells us that God's will is man's well-being everywhere.

We don't have control over a great deal that happens to us in life, but we do have choices to make. We can choose to be self-centered or we can choose to reach outside of ourselves as Mr. Walton does and perform good work. Perhaps we can turn our own misfortunes into something positive.

This is something I firmly believe: because we have all experienced the depth of human suffering, we can empathize and identify with the pain of others. Because the remission of our own pain is so gratefully received, we should be motivated to mitigate the suffering of others. That is my philosophy and really what Aid For Friends is all about.

Everything becomes possible by the
mere presence of someone who knows
how to listen, to live and give of himself.

Elie Weisel

Chapter 21
Harry

Harry was bitter. He had one leg amputated and it was likely the other would go as well. When I visited him for the first time, he was still upset from the accident that caused him to lose his leg.

Harry had always been an active man and he couldn't tolerate being confined to his little apartment. A ramp was built and he looked forward to pushing his wheelchair along the streets of the neighborhood. Then one day the wheelchair tipped over and he wound up lying in the street for what seemed an interminable time until a motorist who narrowly missed running over him rescued him.

Mary volunteered to deliver dinners to Harry and visit with him. She's blessed with an upbeat personality and did her best to cheer him. In addition, a new puppy did wonders for Harry's mental state because he now had something else to think about and be responsible for.

Everything went well until Mary called one day in a panic. Harry had asked her to store his prosthesis because the artificial leg no longer fit him. It was in a long blue storage bag that she had put in the back of her husband's van. Unfortunately, the van was vandalized and robbed that evening. (Can you imagine the thieves' surprise when they took inventory of their booty?) The problem was that the welfare authorities wouldn't pay for a new prosthesis unless he returned the old one. I had a terrible time convincing his social worker's supervisor that an exception should be made in Harry's case. After a week of phone calls, I finally prevailed.

Harry was fitted with a free, new, artificial leg and forgave Mary for the problem that had been inadvertently created. The volunteer found it difficult to interact with Harry sometimes because of his gloomy outlook on life, but her sunny disposition helped maintain the relationship through the years.

Those who bring sunshine to the lives of others cannot keep it from themselves.

Sir James Barrie

Chapter 22
Smiling Mr. DeMarco

K evin and I had difficulty finding the corner row house located in the shadow of Interstate 95. The referring social worker told us to use the rear entrance. After we knocked and waited for a while, a small, stooped figure appeared at the door. Mr. DeMarco let us into his crowded home and I understood why we couldn't enter through the front of the house: it was so crowded with old furniture and the memories of a lifetime that the door was inaccessible.

The elderly gentleman stood before us leaning on his cane. His badly swollen legs made walking extremely difficult. He motioned to us to sit down on a dusty couch and slowly lowered his body onto the chair across from us. There were large photographs (daguerreotypes) of smiling couples in Victorian dress on all of the walls. They gave the little house an eerie quality, as though time had stood still for 80 years.

Mr. DeMarco was witty and charming, his mind a treasury of facts and anecdotes about life in Philadelphia at the turn of the century. He had been a traveling photographer, walking through the streets and alleys of the city soliciting trade.

The shut-in, clad only in his boxer sorts and white tee-shirt because it was hot and humid that day, rose and bade us to follow him. I was astounded as Mr. DeMarco pointed with his cane to a vegetable garden, consisting primarily of tomato plants tied to tall stakes, in the back yard. The man was in his 90s and had congestive heart failure and crippling arthritis. His legs were so badly swollen I couldn't conceive how he was able to plant and tend his garden. But he did! Mr. DeMarco then found a paper bag in a corner of the room and took some ripe tomatoes and peppers from a large bowl. He proudly offered his gift to us. Later that afternoon, I used my share to make delicious spaghetti sauce.

It had been a hectic day but my time spent with Mr. DeMarco didn't seem like work. It was fun! I wished I wasn't so busy with directing Aid For Friends because I really would have enjoyed visiting him each week myself.

A young couple I had recruited as visitor volunteers showed some degree of apprehension about visiting Mr. DeMarco because he was so much older than they. Just one month later, they called and thanked me for the opportunity to explore new horizons, to share, to learn, and to grow as individuals. They felt that they were receiving so much more from Mr. DeMarco than they ever would be able to give. He had charmed them with his wit and twinkling eyes and especially his smile. They had found that they no longer delivered the dinners and visited him as volunteers, but as friends.

If one saves a single life it is as if one saved an entire world.

Sanhedrin IV, 5

Chapter 23
Two Women

I would like to tell you a story about two remarkable women: one, a visitor volunteer, the other, an Aid For Friends client/friend. Their paths would never have crossed nor their precious friendship been forged were it not for Aid For Friends. A suburban home-maker named Loretta read in her local newspaper that I was speaking in her area and she came to find out more about our program. We talked after my presentation and it was quite obvious that she cared about the plight of our homebound clients/friends.

Loretta, a deeply religious woman, told me that she could actualize her faith in service as a volunteer for Aid For Friends. Our new volunteer, along with her friend, Linda, made arrangements for me to speak at their church, and they both offered to act as coordinators for their parish.

Several months later, when Aid For Friends expanded its services to their county, they became outreach coordinators for the entire area. Loretta worked many long hours as all of our outreach coordinators do, but we felt that she should also have personal experience in dealing with a shut-in; therefore, in addition to her role as a county coordinator, she became a visitor to a mentally handicapped woman.

Matilda, the other woman in my story, had an extraordinarily unhappy home life. She was often out of touch with reality because she was a schizophrenic. At times she was delusional and she suffered intensely as do many other individuals with mental illness. Our visitor started bringing her meals, which Matilda thoroughly enjoyed. Her psychiatric case worker felt her improved nutrition and the friendly visiting helped Matilda's condition a great deal. As a result, her psychiatrist was able to decrease both the dosage of her medicine and the number of days spent at the mental health center's day hospital.

Loretta and Matilda spent many hours together and Loretta came to know her friend's distorted view of reality throughout Matilda's vivid hallucinatory descriptions. Our volunteer, a sensitive woman, didn't run away from the pain but instead tried to alleviate her friend's suffering. Sometimes Matilda seemed completely well and Loretta took her shopping at the mall, which they both enjoyed. Loretta is a talented seamstress and she made Matilda a beautiful dress for her birthday. Matilda was so happy with her gift that Loretta knew her efforts made a difference in Matilda's tormented life. Matilda basked in the warm reassurance of love.

Loretta had been visiting Matilda for almost a year when Matilda developed a malignancy; Loretta offered as much comfort as she could in what was to be Matilda's final illness. Matilda died penniless and there was no money to pay for her burial. Loretta, in anguish over losing her dear friend, called other volunteers and local churches. Aid For Friends helped a little, as did many others. A cremation and memorial service were arranged. Loretta, enriched by the relationship, had helped her special friend for the last time. Matilda no longer needed her; she was no longer tormented, but had finally found peace and happiness with the Lord.

The following is from a letter Loretta wrote me after Matilda's death:

"Matilda's illness created a world of delusions. However, these delusions didn't inhibit her function in our society as wife, mother, and friend. She shared her talents of music and her recall of ancient history. She was a very intelligent woman, but because of body chemistry and a childhood environment filled with cruelty, malnutrition, and lack of love, she regressed into a world of make-believe. Yes, Matilda was a child-like adult who needed food, warmth, but most of all love. I thank God for Aid For Friends and the opportunity to serve one of His special children, because I learned how to love and serve my God through Matilda..."

Later that year, on one of WCAU's radio talk shows, I was interviewed about my work with Aid For Friends. The host queried, "Isn't it difficult to get volunteers? I don't think people care about the difficulties of others—strangers. Most people are selfish; they just care about their own little world." I told him that maybe that was *his* experience, but not mine. I am fortunate: I get to know the finest human beings because of my work. I told him about Loretta and Matilda.

But the story I just shared with you isn't extraordinary. There are many generous, unselfish individuals. They don't sit comfortably back in their own little domain, oblivious to the suffering around them, but reach out, make sacrifices if necessary, and through their efforts make life better for shut-ins for perhaps one hour, one day, one year. And for each caring person, that good is compounded and it grows and grows. The world is a better place for it.

He will free the poor man who calls   to
    him, and those who need help.
He will have pity on the poor
    and feeble, and save the lives of those
    in need.

Psalm 72:12-14

Chapter 24

No Food for Mr. Kurtz

There is a man living in this region who, like so many others, cannot survive without Aid For Friends. Mr. Kurtz, a true gentleman who is well mannered and good natured, is inexplicably abused by his wife. Despite the fact that the poor man is a stroke victim and a paraplegic and the couple live together, Mrs. Kurtz will not let him eat any of the food that she purchases. In desperation, Mr. Kurtz called the social worker because the only food his wife gave him was spoiled food that she was going to throw out. He had been eating it because he was so hungry, but he was constantly getting sick.

Mrs. Kurtz does not communicate or interact with her disabled husband in any other way. Such psychological abuse is morally reprehensible! The poor man had nowhere else to live, yet he has found it in his heart to forgive his wife. "She can't cope," he says.

The Aid For Friends dinners, soups, and goodies are his only sustenance. As he gently squeezed my hand, he told me that his visitor is an "angel of mercy." He then gave me a hug and told me that every night he thanks God for sending Aid For Friends to him and asks the Lord to bless all the members of such a wonderful organization. Can you imagine how I felt? Grateful to God that in some small way Aid For Friends could ease this man's suffering:

the suffering from his disabilities, the suffering from his isolation, the suffering from his wife's cruel rejection, and the suffering from hunger. Mr. Kurtz didn't have to verbalize his gratitude; the squeeze from his hand and the hug said volumes. It made my day!

I believe that together we have power. How tragic it would be if we didn't use it. Through God's blessings we have the power to fight suffering. I believe that is a wonderful gift. The definition of power is "the ability to act or produce an effect." Through participation in Aid For Friends or any other nonprofit organization, we have the power to change the lives of the poor, sick, hungry, or homeless.

I am grateful that God has given us the tools to help our fellow man, "the least of these My brothers and sisters." What an opportunity! If we seize the moment and help the sick and disadvantaged who so desperately need us, we can help people like Mr. Kurtz and the others who have yet to call because of the greatest power of all: the power of love! That is a gift that God gives to everyone.

No act of kindness, no matter how small, is ever wasted.

Aesop

Chapter 25
Catherine Volunteers

I remember well when Donna received the referral for Catherine. She had visited Catherine and brought me the list of her ailments and the prescriptions that she must take, which, unbelievably, cost $700–800 monthly. Catherine has combined collagen-vascular disease, which has left her with lupus, diabetes, rheumatoid arthritis, brain damage, and double vision plus other serious and debilitating ailments. She was constantly in and out of the hospital and her many ailments had afflicted her to the extent that she was either in a wheelchair or bed. Catherine was only 52 years old.

We had used emergency funds to help pay for her medicine. The following week, I received a thank you. I called her to thank her for the lovely card. She talked about how delicious the dinners were and how she enjoyed the "goodies" and little cards and notes that are often included. She said it is obvious that the dinners are given with love. Catherine is a religious woman. She did not complain or speak of her pain, but told me she would pray for all of the Aid For Friends helpers.

Out of the blue, three years later, I was surprised to receive the following letter: "Dear Mrs. Schiavone: I am ashamed to think I waited so long to thank you. You are always in my thoughts and I should have written to you sooner. You can never realize how much you have helped me. I can't even imagine what I would have done. Starved, I guess....You have done so much, I wish I could say something more than 'thank you.' 'Thank you' just doesn't do it anymore. The only thing I can do for you is to pray for you and all the volunteers that help you. You are in my prayers and I thank God every day for giving me you. Much love and thanks."

Years passed; the number of client/friends we served increased to more than 1,000; because of the sheer number, I no longer knew them all personally. I hadn't thought about Catherine for many years and then, last month, we recruited an additional 175 volunteers at a church in the far northeast section of Philadelphia.

After I had spoken at the end of Saturday night Mass, a woman came up to me and asked, "Rita, do you remember me?" The frail woman's face was familiar, but I couldn't remember her name or who she was. "See if you remember when I write my name." As she wrote her first name, *Catherine*, the memories flooded back and I gave her a big hug. It was so good to see her.

I couldn't believe that she had been cured and was standing before me, filling out a volunteer card and offering her services as a cook volunteer. We hugged and kissed and then she said, "Rita, more than anyone in this church, I understand how badly you need volunteers and how important Aid For Friends services are to shut-ins. I couldn't have survived without your program. I am doing so much better now and I want to help other shut-ins, so I'll start making meals for Aid For Friends." She made my day!

The following week, I received a letter from Catherine and here is part of it:

> Two years ago, I was down to 65 pounds and couldn't lift my head from the pillow. My doctor told me I would never see Thanksgiving. This was in September. Father O'Hara gave me the Last Rights and by Thanksgiving, I was on my way to recovery.
>
> It has been a long, hard haul. It took me months of hell on earth, but it was certainly worth all the pain. The only explanation the doctor can give me is that the 65 pills a day I was taking were doing all the work—my body was doing nothing—and the complete rest has put the disease in a sort of semiremission. But you know, as I do, that it

was God, love, and prayers from my family and friends and people like you. What would the world be like if no one cared?

I live alone now; it is a blessing for me for I have to depend on myself for everything. I am working and really enjoy it. It is the only office job I've ever had and it is my third time back. I still am under a doctor's care; the collagen disease has come back, but this time I seem to be able to fight it with a better knowledge of what has to be done. I exercise the muscles two or three times a week and find it has helped.

It's funny how things happen. I was cleaning out some papers and I came across an envelope from you. I was so ashamed that with all that has happened, I never wrote or volunteered to help you and your organization. The same week after Mass, who was at the altar but you! God works in many ways. Rita, I don't know how much help I can be to you, but I would like to do something. I am filling the trays and will get more when I drop them off. Rita, 'thank you' just doesn't do it for all that you and the other volunteers do and have been doing for years. You certainly have a place reserved in heaven.

Kindness in words
creates confidence.
Kindness in thinking
creates profoundness.
Kindness in giving
creates love.

Lao Tzu
Chinese Philosopher, 600 BC

Chapter 26

Toni and Martha: Angels

Toni and Martha visited shut-ins for almost 17 years. They worked together at Sears and managed to find time, despite the family obligations of being grandparents, to visit several evenings a week. When they retired, they spent Mondays visiting and caring for sick shut-ins. Through the years they often took their various client-friends on day trips. They shopped, handled banking, and ran errands much to the appreciation and delight of the shut-ins.

One day Toni came to see me for a check to pay for the monthly prescriptions for one of her client-friends, Mrs. Heinz. We had helped to pay for Mrs. Heinz's prescriptions the previous October when I acted as her advocate in securing her assistance. When Mrs. Heinz's monthly rent increased $50, she panicked. Although the PACE program pays for much of each prescription, the shut-in takes 11 different prescribed medicines and the monthly cost is prohibitive.

Toni and Martha helped her in many ways. The meals not only gave her the nutritious dinners that she was not able to prepare herself because of her illness, but they also saved her food dollars. That month the elderly woman was distraught over an outstanding hospital bill of almost $1,000. With Aid For Friends acting as advocate, the hospital graciously and surprisingly forgave the debt—a most unusual occurrence. Mrs. Heinz was so grateful for all that we did for her. I received a card from her in which she wrote, "My words are lost at this time. 'Thank you' is just not enough!"

Toni told me a story about one of their client-friends. They had been visiting Mrs. Cole for about one year. She is in her 80s, has great difficulty walking, lives in a dilapidated house, and is completely isolated. The meals have really helped to restore her health and she has gained weight. Mrs. Cole lives in the past and, although her husband has been dead for almost 20 years, he is still the center of her life. Toni and Martha were concerned because Mrs. Cole did not have a phone, radio, or television. Through the generosity of our volunteer network, we were able to secure a television and radio for her.

Toni laughed as she told me of Mrs. Cole's reaction to Toni and Martha's help through Aid For Friends. She quoted Mrs. Cole verbatim: "Where did you come from? Did God send you? Are you angels?" Patting her tummy, Mrs. Cole referred to the badly needed weight she had gained, saying, "Look at me!"

When I wrote about my meeting with Toni and Martha for our newsletter, Mrs. Cole's words echoed in my mind. "Did God send you? Are you angels?" I think Toni replied, "No, Aid For Friends sent us." But I believe it was God who planted the desire to help, the compassion, and the empathy that motivated Toni and Martha to visit more than 25 shut-ins in the past 17 years. Toni is Roman Catholic; Martha is Presbyterian. They don't merely talk about their faith; they live it. The answer to Mrs. Cole's question about Toni and Martha is yes, they are angels—angels of mercy—and God surely did send them to help the shut-ins.

No one is useless in this
world who lightens the
burden of it to anyone else.

Charles Dickens

Chapter 27

An Extraordinary Couple

I am constantly amazed at the people who volunteer at Aid For Friends. I spoke with Marie, an extraordinary 36-year-old woman, the mother of four young children, including an infant, who told me she thinks Aid For Friends is one of the best charities around. Her husband Al heard me speak at Our Lady of Good Counsel in 1982 and promptly signed up as a volunteer visitor.

He started visiting Anna immediately upon her release from the hospital where she had undergone colostomy surgery for cancer. One week he was too ill to visit her and his wife, who was pregnant with their second child, brought the dinners to Anna. "It was love at first sight," Marie said, "Anna was witty and sweet, a delightful conversationalist."

Anna was an Episcopalian of German origin who loved Italian food when her appetite was hearty. She received and enjoyed Aid For Friends' free meals for seven years.

Anna's cancer metastasized and her condition worsened. She had suffered a traumatic experience many years ago when she was hospitalized in a large ward in the now-closed Philadelphia General Hospital; consequently she was terrified that she might be placed in a nursing home. The young family had grown to love Anna deeply and offered to take her into their home. The invalid's physician suggested the young couple get assistance from Holy Redeemer Visiting Nurse Home Hospice Care. They came daily, bathed her, checked her condition, and monitored her medication and morphine. They also encouraged and offered a great deal of support to the young mother. After two months, Anna went to our Creator. Marie wrote to me.

> Anna was such a good person. She often cared for others during her younger years, rescuing an in-law from skid row, bathing and treating him for lice, caring for him, and nursing him back to health. At the very end, she still had her sense of humor....The experience actually brought our little family closer together. It even brought us closer to our own parents. My mom said she was proud of me. It was difficult at the end. I miss Anna so much. I know she is with Our Lord and her pain is gone. I am sad and then I am happy because I know that when she died, she was not alone and she knew she was loved. I am so grateful to Aid For Friends because otherwise, we never would have met. As soon as I am over her death, I'll start visiting another shut-in.

I said they were an extraordinary couple because, as far as I know, this was the first time visitors from Aid For Friends have actually taken a homebound shut-in into their home to die. Anna must have felt she was in the company of angels.

Tielhard de Chardin wrote, "Some day after we have mastered the winds, the waves, and gravity, we will harness for God the energies of love; and then for the second time in the history of the world, man will have discovered fire." I think that in the past 18 years, Aid For Friends has shown what the love of that extraordinary couple and of others can accomplish. The challenge is not to tire of giving. God continually replenishes the love we give: it is His greatest gift to us and it is never ending. By using God's love in service to others, our personalities take on another dimension and we are better for it.

Do all the good you can,
By all the means you can,
In all the ways you can,
In all the places you can,
At all the times you can,
To all the people you can,
As long as you ever can.

John Wesley's Rule

Chapter 28
Pearl and Stan

One day I went with Cathy to deliver meals to an elderly couple. I was very impressed because the woman was an extraordinarily courageous person. She was stricken with polio when she was nine months old and, although she needed the assistance of crutches all of her life, she wasn't really handicapped.

Pearl worked for many years as a secretary after she graduated from high school. She married a wonderful gentleman and they had many happy years together. Now Pearl has what doctors are calling "post-polio syndrome" and her condition has deteriorated to the point that she can no longer get out of her wheelchair. Her hands are disabled with advanced osteoarthritis. She also has severe vision problems. Her loving husband, Stan, had two strokes and is no longer able to help her except in very limited ways, but their devotion to one another continues unabated.

When Jim and Phyllis, our visitor volunteers, first delivered their dinners, Pearl said there was "instant love." Jim and Phyllis are compassionate, empathetic visitors who have become supportive friends of the shut-ins. They are an example of what makes Aid For Friends so special: caring, loving people. Pearl and Stan are a special couple who have wonderful spirits and are a delight to talk to. They're making the best of a bad situation.

In February the Student Volunteer Committee at Holy Family College held a Sweetheart Luncheon for some of our disabled client-friends and their visitors. Jim and Phyllis brought Pearl and Stan. It was difficult for them to get there, but it was worth it because they had a great time and enjoyed the meal, entertainment, and sing-a-long. The power of positive thinking can get individuals through the most trying of circumstances. Pearl's and Stan's lives can attest to that.

He will free the poor man
who calls to him,
 and those who need help.
He will have pity on the poor
and feeble,
 and save the lives of those
in need.

Psalm 72:12–14

Chapter 29

Two Sisters in a Housing Project

Tina and Betty live in very limited circumstances in a housing project. Betty keeps her little apartment as neat as a pin. Both are disabled by strokes and they have little of this world's goods, but they are rich in love. God's light shines through the constant smile of sweet Tina as she lies in her hospital bed.

When I visited the pair, Tina, who can no longer speak, was able to express herself by jotting down what she wished to say on a paper tablet. Her dedicated sister, Betty, is recovered to the extent that she is able to care for her. The elderly woman must travel 90 minutes by bus to Temple University Hospital's clinic for her own medical care.

The sisters' eyes light up when they talk about their caring visitor, Jim, and the delicious meals and gifts that he brings them. Tina says Jim is her boyfriend. He is a delightful visitor with a very special sense of humor. In his 70s, Jim has been a visitor for 10 years and presently visits six shut-ins. He also helps out at the Aid For Friends Center. (I don't know what we would do without him.) These two sisters have no option but to depend on us. We are fortunate to have the opportunity to serve them.

"Kindness" is the word that came to mind one morning as I lay in bed thinking of the shut-ins I had visited that week; the suffering people of this world need kindness.

One Saturday, Jim, John, and I went again to visit Tina and Betty. They kindly consented to having their pictures taken for the audiovisual presentation Aid For Friends uses for recruiting volunteers. I had brought a pretty glass container of hard candy for Betty and for Tina, coloring books, crayons, and tablets. There was also a beautiful afghan for each of them, hand crocheted by one of our volunteers. They were so happy. Tina, who is unable to sit up in bed, immediately drew a rudimentary sketch of a face for me. She looked up at me, gave me her radiant smile and handed it to me. I thanked her and as I kissed and hugged them goodbye; I thought again what a privilege it is to serve all of the shut-ins.

We are all God's children even though we were born in different circumstances. We may not all look the same, sound the same, or live in the same kind of neighborhood. Some have more than others, not only material things, but other things as well: education, good health, loving friends, and family. Those of us who are more fortunate should help those who need assistance.

The elderly often require very little to make a big difference in their lives. Tina was so pleased to have the crayons, pads, and coloring books. The total cost was perhaps $3.00, but their value to Tina was much greater than that. I believe we should do all we can to show our kindness to the sick who come to Aid For Friends for assistance. Simply feeling sympathy toward those in need does not accomplish anything. The lovely ladies we visited needed concrete assistance. If we make the decision to take the first step and open ourselves in love and sacrifice to serve others, the Lord does the rest.

I know that in my own life I certainly can witness to God's love and help. I have managed to accomplish a great deal in 25 years of community service against what could have been insurmountable odds. I don't say this because I or my accomplishments are astounding. He is wondrous. God gives us the necessary strength and compassion to accomplish what needs to be done. My greatest support is the blessing of an extraordinary husband. Together, we try to make a difference.

Commit everything you do to the
Lord; trust Him to help you and
He will.

Psalm 37:8

Chapter 30
Karl and Matthew: Two Youths

I once received an inquiry form a high school student at Northeast Catholic High School for Boys one afternoon. Karl had read about Aid for Friends' services to the lonely shut-ins and was offering his services as a volunteer. "Is there anyone I can visit?" he asked.

I was not certain how to respond because all of our volunteers were adults. I was amazed when this 16-year-old young man supplied me with a list of references. He was an honor student and was active in the Catholic Youth Organization. His parents were pleased that he wished to help the sick.

There was an elderly woman, a recluse, who was in urgent need of meals and I had no other volunteers available at the time. Mrs. Smith was very poor and lived in a run down home that looked like an old warehouse from so many years of neglect. She lived 15 minutes from Karl's school.

Mrs. Smith had spoken without emotion when our evaluator visited her. She seemed to have lost all interest in living and her responses to questions regarding her needs were perfunctory. I was not certain how she would respond to a teenager, but I felt that she really could not be worse off than she already was. I arranged for Karl to deliver our dinners to the poor woman.

Karl was so good-natured and willing to help. After an introductory period during which he was able to establish his trustworthiness and dependability, they developed a mutually caring relationship.

He offered to sort out the cartons that were stacked throughout Mrs. Smith's home as well as to give the house a good cleaning. He transformed the little place into a livable environment and, because of his genuine affection for Mrs. Smith, she changed as well.

Karl worried about her needs and called me whenever he thought she had a problem that needed attention. The young man started shopping for her weekly; he couldn't do enough for her.

Karl became like a beloved great-grandson to Mrs. Smith, and her depression, brought about by years of absolute isolation, lifted to reveal a woman who still had a sense of humor and who loved to talk about her life. The elderly woman was proud of the fact that she had been one of the first female graduates from the University of Pennsylvania. She was quite articulate and they had long conversations.

Despite the 70-year difference in their ages, the love and respect these two human beings had for one another transcended time and they became very close. Karl, the high school student had truly become a caregiver.

An 11-year-old boy called our office and asked Cathy if he could become a visitor to fulfill his service project promise for Confirmation. Cathy told him he could on the condition that he was always accompanied by a parent. Matthew is of Polish descent and Cathy assigned him to an elderly woman who was born in Poland. Matthew came to the Aid for Friends' Center each week and personally picked out his new friend's dinners. He always asked if any extra "goodies" had come to the Center that he could take to his shut-in. He looked upon the elderly woman as another grandmother and he grew to love her.

When he completed his service requirement he declared to his mother, "I can't give up my lady." That was three years ago. Matthew, an outgoing boy who excels in his studies, graduated from eighth grade in 1993.

These two young men have taken time from their sports, friends, and school activities to serve humanity. At a young age they understand that they should give something back to society. For today's young people, many of whom are caught up in the consumer mode of expensive clothes, sneakers, video games, and whatever else television and peers tell them they need, these two youths are role models.

I shall pass this way but once.
If there is any good deed I can do
or any kindness I can show, let me
not delay, but do it now, for I shall
not pass this way again.

Anonymous

Chapter 31
John Ott's Miracle

So often I read in the newspaper about young people whose lives have been forever ruined by their descent into the drug culture. One of Aid For Friends' finest visitor volunteers is a man in his late 20s who graduated from college with honors. Without his mother's prayers and support, he could have been one of the young men in the headlines.

John stands out in a crowd, not only because of his height, which is six feet, four inches, but because of his demeanor. He is a charismatic individual whose faith has transformed him from an addict into the most sensible, compassionate, loving, and dedicated volunteer a social service agency could ever want.

John was once addicted to alcohol, heroin, and cocaine. The expensive habit forced him to deal drugs and shoplift. He tried private therapy and enrolled in three different drug rehabilitation programs. The young man was no sooner out of that controlled environment when he slipped back into his addictions.

John's mother did not give up hope or reject her son, but continued to pray for a cure. Then a friend invited him to a Catholic charismatic prayer service and Mass. Miraculously, John underwent a conversion experience that evening and walked out of the church a changed person. He started volunteering for various special projects, but kept looking for a program where he could really make a difference.

John heard me speak after Sunday Mass at St. Jerome five years ago and was drawn to our ministry. He volunteered as a visitor and, to be honest, I was skeptical because of his past, but the young man before me was clean cut, well spoken, and courteous. He offered to visit client-friends who were difficult to match with visitors, including AIDS patients who might be referred to us.

John has proven to be an exemplary volunteer visitor—dependable, empathetic, and helpful. In 1988, he volunteered additional time and became an evaluator for us, performing needs assessments and determining the eligibility of referred shut-ins. John became the weekly visitor for three AIDS patients and lovingly ministered to them until their death. He also visited an elderly family and became quite attached to them.

John graduated from Holy Family College and has applied for a position as a teacher. During the summer, in addition to serving as evaluator and visitor, he helps out at the office: cleaning, running errands, and filling in wherever needed.

John was recently honored by his school as Student Volunteer of the Year and for his excellence in studies and leadership. I am so grateful that God sent this special young man to Aid For Friends.

Because John had a checkered past, when he first volunteered I quietly monitored him because I wondered how long he could realistically remain drug free and function as an effective, reliable volunteer. God does work miracles, however, and John's love for his suffering brothers and sisters and the Lord brought about a metamorphosis.

His mother's steadfast faith in her son and her incessant prayers for help were answered; John's future will not be in a crack house or jail, but in a high school, teaching history. Goodness emanates from this special young man and affects everyone with whom he comes in contact. He is a joy!

I have always empathized with people who are addicted to drugs because I smoked four packs of cigarettes daily until recently. I had a chronic cough for many years, but I could not break the nicotine habit. I tried five times to quit, but each time a crisis occurred in my life within six months of quitting. I erroneously thought I could deal with these crises better if I had a cigarette in my hand. My voice had become hoarse, I had trouble breathing, and my blood pressure became dangerously high.

Fear and the grace of God have given me the perseverance to stay away from cigarettes these past four years. Because I could not break my addiction to nicotine for 38 years, I can understand the tremendous effort it must take to break any addiction to alcohol, heroin, and cocaine. God does work wonders!

John's Letter

John visited two sisters and the spouse of one of them. Among the three they had leg ulcers, hip fractures, and senile dementia. I am sharing John's thoughts with you because I believe they encapsulate in a few short paragraphs his strength of character and reverence for the elderly and sick.

Dear Rita:

Sarah, Mike, and Catherine were three of the nicest people I ever met. I often thank God that Aid For Friends allowed me to come into contact with such beautiful people. Sarah and Catherine are adorable twin sisters and Mike is Sarah's husband. Many a happy afternoon we would spend together talking, laughing, and enjoying each other's company. For two and a half years, I delivered meals to these wonderful people and we became very close. My admiration and respect for them increased with each passing week. They displayed a determination and strength that quite humbled me. Their struggle to stay out of a nursing home was a noble fight and it exemplified the finest aspect of human nature: our ability to define who we are through God's grace. Sarah, Mike, and Catherine refused to give in. Their indomitable independence and strength of character awed me.

I wish every young person could experience the noble character of these people. Perhaps they would then share in the admiration that I have for the elderly. We can learn so much from older people, yet what a crime it is that we hide them away, afraid to let the light of their experience, strength, and wisdom shine on our dark world. More than ever do we need that light, for many young people are losing touch with the connecting element of what has gone before us. We live in our own little world in front of our own little televisions, forgetting that we are part of a larger picture. Life is a continuum and the elderly are part of it. They have a very precious and important contribution to make. They connect us to the past, they join us to the larger picture and in this way, they help us to stay in touch with the very essence and fabric of life.

In April of this year, Mike Frazer died. The very same week that he went into the hospital, Catherine McCullum discovered that she could not get out of bed. She, too, went to the hospital. My last visit to their house found Sarah all alone, desperate but still hanging tough. Her life had come crashing down around her in one short week but she still showed that strength that I so much admired. The following week, both Sarah and Catherine were in a nursing home. This particular aspect of their struggle was over. I now visit them at the nursing facility.

I thank God for Aid For Friends. Working with you has given me an education that I could not buy with all the money in the world. The value of your work is inestimable. Cathy, Barbara, Karl, and all the people who contribute to your organization perform an ineffable service to handicapped shut-ins, AIDS victims, and the elderly. I believe that Aid For Friends is divinely inspired and sustained. Without it, many elderly people would be forced to give up their independence and go into nursing homes. Thank God for Aid For Friends.

Sincerely,

John Ott

Founded in 1974
AID FOR
FRIENDS
With Trust In God

Epilogue

The need for Aid For Friends' services continues to grow as the population ages. As of May 1993, the program serves 1,300 of the isolated homebound in the five-county greater Philadelphia area. Most of these shut-ins are very poor. Seven thousand, five hundred volunteers make and donate dinner, drive, visit, coordinate, evaluate, and perform clerical tasks. Three thousand contributors provide more than half of the financial support. Aid For Friends has no guaranteed source of income. The program's support comes from individual contributors, foundations, and corporations.

If you would like to help provide free home-cooked dinners, friendly visiting, supplemental food, advocacy, or emergency financial assistance to the isolated homebound, please call the Aid For Friends office at 215/464-2224 or write to Aid For Friends, 2869 Holme Avenue, Philadelphia, PA 19152-2118.

Aid For Friends is a charitable, nonprofit corporation and has a 501-C-3 with the Internal Revenue Service. Donations are tax deductible. Aid For Friends is also registered with the Pennsylvania State Charitable Commission. A copy of the official registration and financial information may be obtained from the Pennsylvania Department of State by calling toll free, within Pennsylvania, 800/732-0999. Registration does not imply endorsement.

If you are interested in developing a program in other sections of the country using Aid For Friends as a prototype, please contact Rita Ungaro Schiavone at 215/464-2224.